ESCAPING THE MARK OF THE BEAST

By Dr. Terry Gage

Foreword by Dr. Paul Collins

Escaping The Mark Of The Beast
Copyright © 2009 by Dr. Terry Gage

All rights reserved. No part of this book may be reproduced or transmitted in any form or by any means without written permission from the author.

ISBN: 978-0-692-00338-1

Some scripture quotations in this book are from the New American Standard Bible. "Scripture quotations taken from the New American Standard Bible®, Copyright © 1960, 1962, 1963, 1968, 1971, 1972, 1973, 1975, 1977, 1995 by The Lockman Foundation Used by permission." www.Lockman.org These scripture quotations are labeled NASB. All other scripture quotations not so identified are from the King James Version of the Bible.

Printed in the U.S.A.
Biblemystery.com Publishing

Table of Contents

Foreword ………………………………………………	5
Introduction – Escaping the Mark of the Beast …………..	9
Chapter 1 The Bottomless Pit ……………………...........	21
Chapter 2 Mystery Identity of the Beast ………………….	25
Chapter 3 Another Beast ...…………………………….…	33
Chapter 4 The Power of the Beast ………………………...	35
Chapter 5 The Mark of the Beast 666 ..…………………...	39
Chapter 6 Here is Wisdom - Understanding 666 …………	43
Chapter 7 Identity of the Man of Lawlessness ……………	49
Chapter 8 Strong Delusion ………………………………...	53
Chapter 9 Star of Wonder …………………………………	59
Chapter 10 Blood, and Fire, and Vapour of Smoke ……….	67
Chapter 11 Visit from the Cowboy Preacher ……………..	69
Chapter 12 The Mystery of 911 ..…………………………..	73
Chapter 13 The Vision of the Golden Ball ………………..	77
Chapter 14 The Day of the Lord …………………………..	79
Chapter 15 The Kingdom of Heaven Revival ……………..	91
Chapter 16 Sequence of End Time Events ………………..	95
Chapter 17 Babylon the Great - The City ...……………….	107
Chapter 18 Mystery Babylon - A Fallen Angel …………..	115
Chapter 19 The Abomination of Desolation ………………	127
Chapter 20 Left Behind - The Teaching of Jesus …………	135
Chapter 21 Understanding the Seventy Weeks ……………	139
Chapter 22 The Vision of the Two Nails …………………	151
Appendix - Outline for Online Video Teaching …………	155

About the Author
Rev. Terry Gage, M.D.

Dr. Gage graduated from the University of Texas Medical School in Houston in 1979 and has been engaged in the practice of family medicine for 27 years. Through a series of visions from the Holy Spirit in 2001 unique insights into the end time scriptures were developed producing a teaching ministry on radio, the newspaper, television, and through preaching and video DVD presentations. The focus of Dr. Gage's end time message is a call for urgency in evangelistic efforts in our time.

From 1997 to 2001, Dr. Gage served as chairman of the Annual Conference on Incorporating Prayer Into Medical Practice. This conference explored the therapeutic benefits of prayer in medicine and was attended by several hundred physicians and other health care professionals. Dr. Gage continues to pray with patients in the exam room providing the twin blessings of medicine and prayer.

Dr. Gage was ordained by ACTS Ministry in Springfield Missouri on September 11, 2005. He was also named Professor of Eschatology for ACTS Ministry University in 2009 and is currently involved in developing course work for that institution. Dr. Gage also holds the academic position of Associate Clinical Professor of Family and Community Medicine for Texas Tech University Health Sciences Center School of Medicine and is active in teaching medical students.

Dr. Gage is married to Janna, his wife of 33 years. They are blessed with five children David, Amy, Aleah, Jonathan, and Justin who have each contributed important aspects to the development and editing of this book project. Cover design is by Jonathan Gage.

Foreword

Every Christian needs to hear the message God has entrusted to Dr. Terry Gage, M.D. Until you have the privilege of sitting in his audience, the next best thing will be to read his writings. In the field of Bible prophecy, there is no one who comes close to the scholarship demonstrated by Dr. Gage. This man of medicine has an approach to Biblical interpretation that was divinely imparted in a great Charismatic/Pentecostal gathering of Christians who had come together to experience the power of God and the healing ministry of Jesus. Thus, the scripture is alive to the man who was used by the Holy Spirit to be the human author of this book, *Escaping the Mark of the Beast.*

I was privileged to lay hands on Dr. Terry Gage and ordain him as a minister of the Gospel. He is a humble, gentle, loving, and brilliant representative of the Lord Jesus Christ. Acts Ministry is blessed to count him as a member of our clergy.

As I recall, there have been four times that the Holy Spirit has given me a word of knowledge for His servant. Three times, it was followed by a prophecy for him; and he received it graciously and with thanksgiving to be the recipient of God's attention. It is now very evident that our Creator made Dr. Terry Gage to be a special vessel for a unique understanding of the Bible's message for this day in America and the world.

If you think you have read Bible prophecy, think again! If you think you have heard everything about Bible prophecy, think again! I have been in the ministry since January of 1955, and I have heard --- from the mouth of Dr. Gage --- revelation that has been overlooked by the best of the Bible teachers. After 54 years of ministry, and reading multiple volumes on every aspect of prophecy, what my medical friend has written is the best documented material in my experience. College, seminary, and postgraduate studies did not prepare me to minister the truth of the "Last Days." Dr. Gage has become my resource person. I recommend him to you.

Theology has been called "The Queen of the Sciences." The history of the world cannot be taught without considering the history of the church and Christian doctrine. Our western philosophy is steeped in Christianity. The Bible, though controversial to some in academia, continues to be the authority for life and living. The scholarly work directed by the Holy Spirit in Dr. Gage's academic pursuit of truth, will measure up in any debate. Those who deny the validity of Christian scripture will not be able to escape the conclusions drawn by this book. I am convinced it will quickly develop into the definitive textbook to be used for rebuttal of atheistic arguments against God, a sure defense against modern heresies, and one of the Christian's most effective soul-winning handbooks. *Escaping the Mark of the Beast* is a textbook, a handbook, and a source for inspiration and motivation for every Christian daring to read it in its entirety.

The temptation to "hide your head in the sand" must not be allowed to overtake the body of Christ. It is imperative that we pray for our brothers and sisters to be equipped to stand until they are taken away with our Lord in the clouds.

This is a prophetic survey that looks into parts of the Bible from Genesis through Revelation. It is the whole story, the complete picture, and the full gospel. Dr. Gage has been directed by the Holy Spirit to find facts that have been overlooked by other scholars. In my opinion, since the Bible was penned, no man has been enabled to put into writing the detailed accounts pointing prophetically to our day; no man, that is, until now. The author of this book has provided the information you will be thrilled to receive, because *Escaping the Mark of the Beast* is a matter of paramount importance.

This book will enlighten your mind, assist in sealing your heart, open your eyes to truth, and empower you in your confident walk.

You are in for what may be the greatest adventure in reading you have experienced as a Christian. I believe it! Something (or Someone) inside me is whispering, "Yes, it is true. They will read, arise, and be blessed."

Isaiah 60:1 says, "Arise, shine, for your light has come, and the glory of the Lord rises upon you" (NIV). I heard these words over and over in my mind after attending a seminar to "study at the feet" of Oral Roberts. I hear the same message when I listen to Dr. Terry Gage. Until you can hear him speak in person, keep this book next to your favorite chair where you like to sit and listen to the voice of the Spirit. You will receive God's revelation every time you open its pages. Take it with you on trips. Read it on airplanes and in hotel rooms. Live with and in this book. God is ready to prepare you for the end of time as we have known it. Become the expert your family needs.

I have taken a lot of space --- and your time --- to reach a very simple conclusion. Here it is. Read this book diligently, prayerfully, and as directed by the Holy Spirit. The times are extremely challenging, and the challenges will increase in severity. One translation of Holy Scripture says that "without knowledge, God's people perish." There is another reference that says "without a vision, people perish." Dr. Terry Gage has been obedient to write down much of what the Holy Spirit has revealed to him regarding our future as Christians. He has placed knowledge of "End Times" at our fingertips. He has scholarly opened academic windows to clarify our vision.

My friend, Dr. Gage, has spent hundreds and hundreds of hours of research and writing so we can spend just a few to know God's plan for us as shown in His word.

Dr. Paul Collins, M.Div., Th.D.
Founder, Acts Ministry

Introduction - Escaping the Mark of the Beast

<u>Escaping the Mark of the Beast,</u> sound like the title for an exciting novel? No. This is real.

The beast is real. His mark of eternal destruction is real. This is not a novel. Survival will depend on escaping the mark of the beast. The way of escape from the mark of the beast is clearly defined in this book. The great mysteries, the identity of the beast, and many specifics of the book of Revelation are solved and detailed here.

I have a brother in Christ who proclaims this entire message much more powerfully, prophetically, and simply than I am able. His name is Johnny Landrum. Johnny stands for something. He stands all day long on a busy street corner in Lubbock, Texas holding a sign. Johnny's sign does not say, "THE END IS NEAR" though that would be accurate. Instead the sign proclaims the way of escape from the coming mark of the beast. All day long Johnny stands with his sign on a busy street corner. People honk. People stare. They stare at Johnny and his sign. Johnny's hand painted sign boldly proclaims in blood red letters…

JESUSAVESOULS

At the direction of the Lord, Johnny stands at this particular street corner. He holds his sign from **6** am to **6** pm **6** days a week, on **66**th street and the **66**00 block of University across the street from the Phillips **66** station.

The story of how Johnny arrived at this particular street corner several months ago reveals a special prophetic significance about escaping the mark of the beast. Johnny's sign shows the way of escape. All day long Johnny never sits, he continuously stands holding his sign…

JESUSAVESOULS

For over five months Johnny has been standing, never sitting, holding his sign. Like a silent sentinel Johnny stands hour after hour, day after day, week after week, and month after month proclaiming the only way of escaping the mark of the beast.

Johnny's story was detailed in the local newspaper on the front page January 11, 2009. You can read more about him and see a video clip about Johnny at the website address…
http://www.lubbockonline.com/stories/011109/loc_376111280.shtml

Johnny is real. His message is real. This is not a novel.

The supernatural events that moved Johnny to that particular corner with his sign are also real. Last summer the Lord moved Johnny to give away his possessions, even his pickup truck. He gave it to a man who needed a way to get to work. In Johnny's empty garage were some boards on which he painted a sign with red paint. The sign proclaims the way of escape… JESUSAVESOULS.

For three days he took the sign into stores and businesses proclaiming his message JESUSAVESOULS. Some clapped, many stared, and managers ushered him out. When three joyous days were finished he went home and tossed the sign into the dumpster. The garbage truck came and went, but a week later when Johnny went to empty more trash he found the sign still in the dumpster. Johnny took the sign out and he heard the Lord directing him to go to a street corner. He went to 34th Street and Quaker Avenue and there he stood with the sign for three more days. When those three days were finished, he went home and once again tossed the sign into the dumpster. The garbage truck came and went, but a week later when Johnny went to empty more trash he found the sign still in the dumpster.

Johnny said, "It's a sign."

What would you say?

The Lord then directed Johnny to 66th Street and University Avenue. He has been there now for over 5 months every Sunday through Friday. The Lord said he is to be off on Saturdays to rest.

No matter the weather Johnny stands. Whether the temperature is a sultry 95 degrees in August, or a frigid windy 22 degrees in January, it does not matter. Johnny stands with his sign from **6** am to **6** pm **6** days a week, on **66**th street and the **66**00 block of University across the street from the Phillips **66** station. His sign proclaims the way of escape from the coming mark of the beast. It is a sign.

JESUSAVESOULS

I recently met Johnny and his partner, a 22 year old man named Celestino. Celestino's car broke down on 66th Street where he met Johnny. The Lord has called Celestino along side to help Johnny. It is an answer to prayer. They stand together and hold the sign. They sing together and dance before the Lord together in praise. It is an answer to prayer. They stand. They never sit. Johnny and Celestino are standing before the Lord of the earth as two witnesses proclaiming the way of escape from the coming mark of the beast. Their presence on that street corner on 66th street from 6 am to 6 pm 6 days a week is a sign. It is a sign. The mark of the beast is coming, and the only way of escape is *"the way, the truth, and the life." **John 14:6***

JESUSAVESOULS

One Sunday the Lord moved me to serve Johnny and Celistino communion, the Lord's supper. I asked Johnny if anyone had ever brought them communion. No one had, but they, along with the newspaper salesman hawking papers on the same street corner, joined me as we prayed. We thanked the Lord for the bread, His body broken for us, and for the cup, the New Testament in His blood shed for the forgiveness of sins. We partook together in remembrance of Jesus Christ and what He did for us on the cross. By doing so we were fulfilling the scripture which speaks of the Lord's supper, *"proclaiming the Lord's death until He comes." **1 Corinthians 11:26***

As I went back to my pickup Johnny caught me and said, "The Lord wants you to know, 'Don't run from your calling.'" Just in case you would like to know, that is why I am writing this book. You could say that Johnny put me up to it. If Johnny can do what he does at the direction of the Lord, I can try one more time to finish this book. After all, the presence of Johnny and Celestino at that street corner with that sign is a sign.

It is a sign.

I shared with Johnny some of the prophetic mysteries contained in the book you are holding. I shared with him the deeper meanings of 666, how the number six symbolizes coming destruction in the Bible, the name and identity of the beast, the coming destruction of the mark of the beast, and why the Lord placed him at that particular corner.

Johnny seemed to already know or easily understand these things, but was greatly encouraged to know more about the prophetic meaning of his service which takes place from 6 am to 6 pm 6 days a week. After all the temperature was 22 degrees and dark this morning at 6 am when Johnny arrived at his designated street corner before much traffic had begun to flow. But Johnny doesn't care about the weather. He knows precisely what the Lord told him to do and he precisely does it. That is all.

Johnny told me that my sharing of these things almost brought tears to his eyes. Then looking up, he humbly and gratefully said, "Of all the people why would the Lord pick me for this?"

There is much more to Johnny's story about others stopping to bring Johnny food, or gloves, or hats, or cash, and how Johnny uses a little for his daily needs and gives the rest away. There is much more to say about Johnny's piercing spiritual eyes, his welcoming smile, and about his quiet and gentle voice, but you can read more about it in the newspaper's website.

I have another brother in Christ, a friend of many years, whose story must be told. His name is Steve Mann. Ten years ago Steve had a prophetic dream. Acts chapter 2 tells of dreams and visions which shall come to man near the time of the impending day of the Lord.

Acts 2:17 *And it shall come to pass in the last days, saith God, I will pour out of my Spirit upon all flesh: and your sons and your daughters shall prophesy, and your young men shall see visions, and your old men shall dream dreams:*

In Steve's dream the Lord revealed the totally unexpected events that will suddenly take place on the Day of the Lord at the return of Jesus Christ. Steve's dream was a catalyst which opened up my mind's inquiry of the Lord regarding the mysteries in the book of Revelation. The unusual supernatural events leading up to the dream are real. This is not a novel.

Steve works in a hospital business office containing a number of individual work cubicles as well as a lot of hustle and bustle. Late one afternoon the office was totally quiet. Steve glanced at his watch. Strangely quiet for 4 pm. Steve looked around and noticed that everyone was gone. Had the rapture occurred? Had he missed it?

The cleaning lady pushed her cart around the corner, "Mr. Steve. You are working late tonight? It's after 5."

Steve glanced at his watch again. It had stopped at 4 pm. The battery had gone out one might suppose. Steve went home and failing to find a replacement battery came across a spare watch that was keeping time and put it on his wrist.

The next afternoon Steve's office again became strangely quiet. Steve glanced at his watch. It had stopped at about 4 pm. Quitting time had come and gone and Steve was once again 'Left Behind.'

Steve stopped on the way home to buy a new watch battery and put it in. The watch ran for one hour, then stopped. Steve walked into the living room of his home. Glancing at the mantle above the fireplace he noticed that the movement on the mantle clock had stopped. Steve stared at the frozen clock with wonder.

"What is going on?" Steve thought.

Scratching his head he walked into his computer room to work for a while before bedtime. He glanced at the clock on his desk. Guess what? His desk clock had stopped.

"Is this a sign?" Steve thought.

What would you think? It was a sign.

Steve went to bed and prayed, "Lord. What is it with the time, and all of my clocks stopping?" He then fell asleep. The dream began suddenly with the voice of the Lord…

"THE TIME HAS COME FOR THE DESTRUCTION OF ALL EVIL ON THE EARTH."

Steve found himself walking on a sidewalk on a beautiful afternoon. Everything was peaceful. The air was calm, the sun warm and bright. Suddenly the wind began to blow, the earth under Steve's feet began to tremble, and the sky became dark. There was sheer terror everywhere. People were running and screaming. Steve said the feeling of terror was unlike anything he had ever experienced. It was a combination of deep terror and total hopelessness. A great wind was causing leaves and debris to fly everywhere. People were screaming and falling down with fear as the sky grew darker and the earth shook more violently.

Steve ran into a building, which looked like a hospital, and entered a small room. The room was empty and the walls were pure white. Steve crouched in the corner covering his head with his arms in terror. The fear was so intense that he could not speak but instead began to cry because of the terror. Finally Steve was able call on the name of Jesus…

"Jesus, Jesus, Jesus! Jesus cover me with your blood!" Steve then began to pray in the Spirit.

Steve had called on the name of the Lord and just as suddenly, he was in a vehicle with an angel being transported far away from the destruction. Steve had escaped the destruction that was coming upon the earth. He was taken <u>out of tribulation</u> which had just begun upon the earth.

In this dream Steve experienced the events of the day of the Lord. The sun went dark. The earth shook. Great fear came upon all who were dwelling on the earth. Steve called on the name of Jesus and was taken <u>out of great tribulation</u> to <u>stand</u> in a great multitude <u>before the Lord</u> at the throne. These events describe what shall take place on the day of the Lord and are described in Revelation chapters 6 & 7 at the opening of the sixth seal.

Revelation 6:12 *And I beheld when he had opened the <u>sixth seal</u>, and, lo, there was a <u>great earthquake</u>; and the <u>sun became black</u> as sackcloth of hair…*

Revelation 6:15 *And the kings of the earth, and the great men, and the rich men, and the chief captains, and the mighty men, and every bondman, and every free man, <u>hid themselves</u> in the dens and in the rocks of the mountains;* ***16*** *And said to the mountains and rocks, Fall on us, and hide us from the face of him that sitteth on the throne, and from the wrath of the Lamb:* ***17*** *For the great <u>day of his wrath</u> is come; and who shall be able to stand?*

The great <u>day of His wrath</u> is also known as the great and notable <u>day of the Lord</u>. Note carefully that those <u>left behind</u> hiding in caves and rocks are not in doubt as to what is taking place. They are not scratching their heads questioning the meaning of the disappearance of those taken in the rapture. They will not think the rapture is an alien abduction. No. <u>Every eye shall see Him</u>, the Lord Jesus Christ coming on the clouds in power and glory as He sends his angels to gather the elect. Those left behind shall not say, "Why did they all disappear?" Instead, they shall say, "<u>Hide us</u> from the face of him that sitteth on the throne."

Revelation 1:7 *Behold, he cometh with clouds; and <u>every eye shall see him</u>, and they also which pierced him: and <u>all kindreds of the earth shall wail</u> because of him. Even so, Amen.*

In Steve's dream he was being transported away from the destruction of tribulation beginning on the earth to a safe destination. The following scripture describes that destination.

***Revelation 7:9** After this I beheld, and, lo, a great multitude, which no man could number, of all nations, and kindreds, and people, and tongues, **<u>stood</u>** before the throne, and **<u>before the Lamb</u>**, clothed with white robes, and palms in their hands; **10** And cried with a loud voice, saying, Salvation to our God which sitteth upon the throne, and unto the Lamb. **11** And all the angels stood round about the throne, and about the elders and the four beasts, and fell before the throne on their faces, and worshipped God, **12** Saying, Amen: Blessing, and glory, and wisdom, and thanksgiving, and honour, and power, and might, be unto our God for ever and ever. Amen. **13** And one of the elders answered, saying unto me, What are these which are arrayed in white robes? and whence came they? **14** And I said unto him, Sir, thou knowest. And he said to me, These are they which <u>came out of great tribulation</u>, and have washed their robes, and made them white in the blood of the Lamb.*

In Steve's dream, he <u>came out of great tribulation</u> as he was raptured away from destruction. Steve did not stay in tribulation to be martyred, as is the common interpretation of Revelation 7:9-14. No, he came out of great tribulation. He escaped to stand before the Son of man. The great multitude *"which no man could number"* in the above scripture passage is not a multitude of tribulation martyrs. No! The raptured church is the make up of this great multitude *"which no man could number."* These arrive at the throne room of heaven, escaping the earth to stand before the Son of man, as the tribulation begins on the day of the Lord.

A stumbling block for many Bible scholars is the false vision of a myriad of "tribulation martyrs." Some of the scriptures these scholars point to in support of their view are actually explained by the death of those martyred for Christ in all the centuries prior to tribulation. Other scriptures they cite are actually fulfilled and explained by the death of <u>just the two witnesses</u>. With the exception of the two witnesses there shall be no martyrs killed during tribulation. Scriptural documentation of this fact is presented throughout the remainder of this book, one example of which is found on pages 99-100.

In Luke chapter 21 Jesus warned of the need to be ready for the escape to stand before Him.

Luke 21:36 *Watch ye therefore, and pray always, that ye may be accounted worthy **to escape** all these things that shall come to pass, and **to stand before the Son of man**.*

Acts chapter two tells the way of escape on the day of the Lord that comes by calling on the name of Jesus. It speaks of the events of the day of the Lord as the sun goes dark and the moon turns blood red in the face of, or before, that great and notable day of the Lord.

Acts 2:20 THE <u>SUN SHALL BE TURNED INTO **DARKNESS**</u> AND THE MOON INTO BLOOD, BEFORE THAT GREAT AND NOTABLE DAY OF THE LORD. **21** AND IT SHALL COME TO PASS, THAT <u>WHOSOEVER SHALL CALL ON THE NAME OF THE LORD SHALL BE SAVED</u>.

Shortly thereafter the Lord revealed to Steve a scripture also describing <u>the day of the Lord</u> he had experienced in his dream. The scripture describes the coming day of the Lord.

Zephaniah 1:14 *The great <u>day of the LORD</u> is near, it is near, and hasteth greatly, even the voice of the day of the LORD: the mighty man shall cry there bitterly. **15** That day is a day of wrath, a day of trouble and distress, a day of wasteness and desolation, a day of <u>darkness</u> and gloominess, a day of clouds and thick <u>darkness</u>, **16** A day of the trumpet and alarm against the fenced cities, and against the high towers. **17** And I will bring distress upon men, that they shall walk like blind men, because they have sinned against the LORD: and their blood shall be poured out as dust, and their flesh as the dung. **18** Neither their silver nor their gold shall be able to deliver them in the day of the LORD'S wrath; but the whole land shall be devoured by the fire of his jealousy:*

*for he shall make even a speedy riddance of **all** them that dwell in the land.*

After Steve told me about his dream, the Lord sent me a vision that was key to understanding all the mysteries in the book of Revelation. In this vision the Lord showed me four perfect red apples lifted upon a table or platform. And below were two fallen apples, bad and rotten apples. The four good apples represent the four angelic beasts which John saw praising God around the throne in Revelation chapter four.

Revelation 4:6 *And before the throne there was a sea of glass like unto crystal: and in the midst of the throne, and round about the throne, were <u>four beasts</u> full of eyes before and behind. **7** And the first beast was like a lion, and the second beast like a calf, and the third beast had a face as a man, and the fourth beast was like a flying eagle. **8** And the four beasts had each of them six wings about him; and they were full of eyes within: and they rest not day and night, saying, Holy, holy, holy, Lord God Almighty, which was, and is, and is to come.*

The four angelic beasts seen by John are very powerful and central in the Kingdom of Heaven. But long ago, before Lucifer's rebellion in heaven, there were originally <u>six</u> angelic beasts surrounding the throne with praise. Scripture tells us that Lucifer, who rebelled and became Satan, drew down 1/3 of all the angels in rebellion.

The two bad apples in my vision represented 1/3 of an original six angelic beasts. These two bad angelic beasts represent the 1/3 who fell and were cast out of heaven, while the four good angelic beasts remain around the throne in heaven.

These bad angelic beasts are so bad and so powerful that they are concealed today, locked up in a prison for fallen angels deep within the earth. That prison is called the <u>bottomless pit</u>.

The two fallen angelic beasts <u>were</u> at the throne, and <u>now they are not</u>. Someday they will <u>ascend from the bottomless pit</u>, and will ultimately go into perdition. This is the solution to the great mystery of the beast in Revelation 17:8.

Revelation 17:8 *"The beast that thou sawest <u>was, and is not;</u> and shall ascend out of the bottomless pit, and go into perdition:"*

Take your finger and point down. You are pointing to a place deep within the earth that the Bible calls the bottomless pit. It is a prison for the worst of the worst of the fallen angels. You are pointing at the two fallen angelic beasts and their hoard of scorpion demons as described in Revelation chapter 9.

We are told there that the king over the scorpion demons is Abaddon, or Apollyon (the destroyer in the Greek.) Apollyon, the angel of the bottomless pit is a fallen angelic beast. This beast will direct his army of scorpion demons on missions of torture across the earth.

Revelation 9:6 *And in those days shall men seek death, and shall not find it; and shall desire to die, and death shall flee from them.*

Ever have heard the phrase, "When all hell breaks loose?" On the day of the Lord when the Lord comes and evacuates his people at the event of the rapture of the Church, the bottomless pit will be opened. Then, "All hell will break loose" as the bottomless pit is opened. The two fallen angelic beasts will ascend from the bottomless pit and bring total domination and ultimate destruction to those left behind on the earth.

In Luke chapter 21 Jesus describes that coming day of the Lord as a snare coming upon all them that dwell on the face of the whole earth. Escape will take place for those who are accounted worthy because they have received forgiveness through the cleansing blood of Jesus. They will escape the earth to stand before the Lord who is in heaven at the right hand of the Father. This event of escape, commonly called the rapture, is described by Jesus in Luke chapter 21 as an <u>escape to stand before Him</u> at the throne in heaven. This event is also seen in Revelation chapter 7.

Luke 21:34 *And take heed to yourselves, lest at any time your hearts be overcharged with surfeiting, and drunkenness, and cares of this life, and so that day come upon you unawares. **35** For as a snare shall it come on all them that dwell on the face of the whole earth. **36** Watch ye therefore, and pray always, that ye may be accounted worthy <u>to escape</u> all these things that shall come to pass, and <u>to stand before the Son of man</u>.*

Revelation 7:9 *After this I beheld, and, lo, a great multitude, which no man could number, of all nations, and kindreds, and people, and tongues, <u>stood</u> before the throne, and <u>before the Lamb</u>, clothed with white robes, and palms in their hands;*

The Kingdom of Heaven is at hand, and we are about to see the return of the King of Kings and Lord of Lords. The purpose of this book is not to entertain but rather to prepare you with knowledge of the word of God and encourage your efforts in evangelism.

The main body of this book is written in a format similar to a teaching workbook or study guide on the book of Revelation. As a medical school professor I am aware that certain formats and teaching strategies can assist in conveying complex information with improved comprehension.

The reader is invited to view the many underlined words in the text as clues to the answers of future test questions much like a study guide prepared for an upcoming final examination. This strategy facilitates greater understanding of the many detailed and complex mysteries solved in this book. But of greater importance is the very simple and powerful truth proclaimed by Johnny Landrum and his sign.

It is a sign…

JESUSAVESOULS

Chapter 1 The Bottomless Pit

The bottomless pit is a recurring theme in the book of Revelation. It is an important key to understanding not only the nature and identity of the beast, but also the grave importance of finding the way of escape from the mark of the beast.

At the onset of tribulation the bottomless pit shall be opened. The sun shall be <u>darkened</u> by smoke from the pit.

Revelation 9:2 *And he opened the bottomless pit; and there arose a smoke out of the pit, as the smoke of a great furnace; and the <u>sun and the air were darkened</u> by reason of the smoke of the pit.*

Note in the following scripture that <u>the day of the Lord</u> is a day of <u>darkness</u>. The darkness on the day of the Lord occurs as the bottomless pit is opened as described in the scripture above.

Zephaniah 1:14 *The great day of the LORD is near, it is near, and hasteth greatly, even the voice of the day of the LORD: the mighty man shall cry there bitterly.* **15** *That day is a day of wrath, a day of trouble and distress, a day of wasteness and desolation, a day of <u>darkness</u> and gloominess, a day of clouds and thick <u>darkness</u>…*

On that great and notable day of the Lord, judgment shall come as a snare upon all those left behind dwelling upon the earth as tribulation begins. The sun shall go <u>dark</u>, the moon shall turn blood red, and the entire earth shall shake with a great earthquake. The beast shall be released to ascend out of the bottomless pit to bring domination and damnation to all those left behind.

On that great and notable day of the Lord, it shall come to pass that <u>whosoever shall call on the name of the Lord shall be saved</u> in the escape of the rapture of the Church. Those who are left behind will take the beast's mark of eternal destruction. All those who call on the name of Jesus shall escape these things that shall come to pass and stand before the Son of man.

JESUSAVESOULS

The following scriptures describe the bottomless pit in the book of Revelation.

Revelation 9:1*And the fifth angel sounded, and I saw a star fall from heaven unto the earth: and to him was given the key of the <u>bottomless pit</u>. **2** And he opened the <u>bottomless pit</u>; and there arose a smoke out of the <u>pit</u>, as the smoke of a great furnace; and the sun and the air were darkened by reason of the smoke of the <u>pit</u>.*

Revelation 9:11*And they had a king over them, which is the angel of the <u>bottomless pit</u>, whose name in the Hebrew tongue is Abaddon, but in the Greek tongue hath his name Apollyon.*

Note: In the above passage that Abaddon, aka Apollyon, shall ascend out of the bottomless pit. He is <u>the beast</u> who shall ascend out of the bottomless pit. He is a <u>fallen angelic beast</u>, an angel of great power.

Revelation 11:3*And I will give power unto my two witnesses, and they shall prophesy a thousand two hundred and threescore days, clothed in sackcloth...**Revelation 11:7****And when they shall have finished their testimony, <u>the beast that ascendeth out of the bottomless pit</u> shall make war against them, and shall overcome them, and kill them.*

Revelation 17:8*The beast that thou sawest was, and is not; and <u>shall ascend out of the bottomless pit</u>, and go into perdition:*

Revelation 20:1*And I saw an angel come down from heaven, <u>having the key of the bottomless pit</u> and a great chain in his hand.**2** And* *he laid hold on the dragon, that old serpent, which is the Devil, and Satan, and bound him a thousand years, 3 And cast him into the <u>bottomless pit, and shut him up</u>, and set a seal upon him, that he should deceive the nations no more, till the thousand years should be fulfilled:*

In the above passage, the bottomless pit is described as a prison for Satan during the 1000 year reign of Christ on the earth. This millennial reign of Christ shall occur after the beast is cast into the lake of fire at the end of tribulation.

This is the same bottomless pit that is currently holding the beast Abaddon also known as Apollyon. This fallen angelic beast has been imprisoned in the bottomless pit since the initial rebellion of Satan in heaven.

While Satan has spent thousands of years roaming the earth like a roaring lion seeking whom he may devour, the beast Apollyon is so bad and so powerful that he has been confined in the prison for fallen angels known as the bottomless pit. The beast, Apollyon "the destroyer," shall be released to ascend out of the bottomless pit at the onset of the tribulation period when the bottomless pit is opened.

Chapter 2 Mystery Identity of the Beast

The beast... "was, and is not; and shall ascend out of the bottomless pit." Revelation 17:8

Revelation 11:3 And I will give power unto my <u>two witnesses</u>, and they shall prophesy a thousand two hundred and threescore days, clothed in sackcloth. 4 These are the two olive trees, and the two candlesticks <u>standing before the God</u> of the earth. 5 And if any man will hurt them, fire proceedeth out of their mouth, and devoureth their enemies: and if any man will hurt them, he must in this manner be killed. 6 These have power to shut heaven, that it rain not in the days of their prophecy: and have power over waters to turn them to blood, and to smite the earth with all plagues, as often as they will. 7 And when they shall have finished their testimony, the **<u>beast that ascendeth out of the bottomless pit</u>** *shall make war against them, and shall overcome them, and kill them.*

We also know from Revelation chapter 9 the fallen angel who ascends out the bottomless pit is named Abaddon or Apollyon. This angel is the beast that ascends out of the bottomless pit. He is a fallen <u>angelic beast</u>.

Understanding the identity of the beast is key to a clear understanding of the book of Revelation. The beast shall ascend out to the bottomless pit. The bottomless pit is a prison for fallen angels. The beast is a fallen angel. He is a fallen angelic beast.

The identity of the beast is not a matter of conjecture or speculation. The name of the beast is specifically identified in scripture in Revelation 9:11. The beast is not human. The beast is a <u>fallen angel</u> and specifically is a fallen angelic beast, a fallen counterpart of the four angelic beasts described in Revelation chapter 4.

When Satan rebelled and drew down 1/3 of the angelic host there were originally six angelic beasts surrounding the throne with praise.

Two angelic beasts, or 1/3 of an original six angelic beasts, followed Satan in rebellion. These two bad beasts are currently locked in the bottomless pit, a prison for fallen angels.

The other four good angelic beasts, that were seen by John, remain around the throne. The angelic beasts have an amazing appearance and powerful ministry.

Revelation 4:6 *And before the throne there was a sea of glass like unto crystal: and in the midst of the throne, and round about the throne, were <u>four beasts</u> full of eyes before and behind. **7** And the first beast was like a lion, and the second beast like a calf, and the third beast had a face as a man, and the fourth beast was like a flying eagle. **8** And the four beasts had each of them six wings about him; and they were full of eyes within: and they rest not day and night, saying, Holy, holy, holy, Lord God Almighty, which was, and is, and is to come.*

The power and physical appearance of the four angelic beasts is amazing and would cause anyone to <u>wonder</u> in amazement should they behold these beasts. Likewise the appearance of the fallen angelic beast who arises out of the bottomless pit shall cause those who dwell on the earth to <u>wonder</u> when they behold him.

Revelation 17:8 <u>*The beast that thou sawest*</u> *was, and is not; and shall ascend out of the bottomless pit, and go into perdition: and <u>they that dwell on the earth shall</u> **wonder**, whose names were not written in the book of life from the foundation of the world, <u>when they behold the beast</u> that was, and is not, and yet is.*

The physical description of the fallen angelic beast is given in Revelation chapter 13.

Revelation 13:2 *And <u>the beast which I saw</u> was like unto a leopard, and his feet were as the feet of a bear, and his mouth as the mouth of a lion...*

Like other angelic beasts, this angelic beast has an amazing appearance. Those who dwell on the earth shall see the amazing appearance of the beast and <u>wonder</u> when they behold him.

An excellent piece of art depicts this beast, this angel of the bottomless pit released on the day of the Lord as the bottomless pit is opened. The painting is by Pat Marvenko Smith and can be viewed at the website http://www.revelationillustrated.com/shop/image14.asp

The painting at the above website is entitled FIRST SIX TRUMPET JUDGEMENTS and is print #14 in the Revelation Series at the website www.revelationillustrated.com

As you view this painting of the angel of the bottomless pit whose name is Apollyon can you imagine any unsaved human being able to face him and refuse his mark?

The beast shall not inhabit or hide in the shell of a human being. He shall appear to the inhabitants of the earth in his actual amazing form, and shall thus deceive and also force by his great power <u>all</u> the inhabitants of the earth to worship him and take his mark. The word <u>all</u> means all. That is why escape in the rapture is the essential factor in escaping the mark of the beast.

Revelation 13:16 *And he causeth **<u>all</u>**, both small and great, rich and poor, free and bond, to receive a mark in their right hand, or in their foreheads…*

Those whose names were written in the book of life from the foundation of the world shall <u>escape</u> to <u>stand</u> before the Son of man before the throne in heaven at the event of the rapture. All those who are <u>left behind</u> shall be those whose names <u>were not written in the book of life</u> from the foundation of the world.

These left behind will be those dwelling on the earth when the beast arises from the bottomless pit at the initiation of tribulation. They shall wonder <u>when they behold the beast</u> that was, and is not, and yet is. Look at the passage again with this key to understanding in mind.

Revelation 17:8 *The beast that thou sawest was, and is not; and shall ascend out of the bottomless pit, and go into perdition: and they that dwell on the earth shall wonder, <u>whose names were not written in the book of life from the foundation of the world</u>, when they behold the beast that was, and is not, and yet is.*

The lost shall behold the beast and wonder. <u>The saved shall not behold the beast</u> for they shall be taken away in the escape of the rapture on the day the beast is released from the bottomless pit.

The identity and the actual name of the beast is clearly defined in scripture, but has been concealed from our understanding until now near the time of the end. The name of the beast is <u>Abaddon,</u> or in the Greek <u>Apollyon.</u> That name means "the <u>destroyer</u>" or "<u>destruction</u>." This name is given in Revelation 9:11 and is identified also as "<u>the angel of the bottomless pit</u>." The following passage describes the events at the opening of the bottomless pit at the initiation of the tribulation period.

Revelation 9:1 *And the fifth angel sounded, and I saw a star fall from heaven unto the earth: and to him was given the key of the bottomless pit.* **2** *And he opened the bottomless pit; and there arose a smoke out of the pit, as the smoke of a great furnace; and the sun and the air were darkened by reason of the smoke of the pit.* **3** *And there came out of the smoke locusts upon the earth: and unto them was given power, as the scorpions of the earth have power.* **4** *And it was commanded them that they should not hurt the grass of the earth, neither any green thing, neither any tree; but only those men which have not the seal of God in their foreheads.* **5** *And to them it was given that they should not kill them, but that they should be tormented five months: and their torment was as the torment of a scorpion, when he striketh a man.* **6** *And in those days shall men seek death, and shall not find it; and shall desire to die, and death shall flee from them.* **7** *And the shapes of the locusts were like unto horses prepared unto battle; and on their heads were as it were crowns like gold, and their faces were as the faces of men.* **8** *And they had hair* *as the hair of women, and their teeth were as the teeth of lions.* **9** *And they had breastplates, as it were breastplates of iron; and the sound of their wings was as the sound of chariots of many horses running to battle.* **10** *And they had tails like unto scorpions, and there were stings in their tails: and their power was to hurt men five months.* **11** *And they had a king over them, which is the angel of the bottomless pit, whose name in the Hebrew tongue is Abaddon, but in the Greek tongue hath his name Apollyon.*

The beast is not a man, a government, a system, a nation, or a computer. The beast is a fallen angelic spirit. This angelic beast is currently concealed in the bottomless pit, to later be revealed in his time. This fallen angelic beast is currently imprisoned in the same bottomless pit that Satan will one day in the future be locked up in for 1000 years. The angel of the bottomless pit, known as Apollyon the beast, is a <u>spirit of antichrist</u> who shall come upon the earth when the bottomless pit is opened.

The beast is a spirit of antichrist. All angels are spirits. All fallen angels are spirits. All fallen angels are spirits of antichrist.

*1 John 4:3 And <u>every</u> **<u>spirit</u>** that confesseth not that Jesus Christ is come in the flesh is not of God: and this is that **<u>spirit of antichrist</u>**, whereof ye have heard that <u>it should come</u>; and even now already is in the world.*

Antichrist is not a man but rather a <u>spirit</u>. A spirit of antichrist is a fallen <u>angel</u>.

*1 John 2:18 Little children, it is the last time: and as ye have heard that **<u>antichrist shall come</u>**, even now are there many antichrists; whereby we know that it is the last time.*

Many antichrist spirits (fallen angels) are present on the earth <u>now</u>. Another spirit of antichrist is prophesied to come forth onto the earth in the <u>future</u>.

The spirit of antichrist prophesied to come to the earth in the future is a fallen angelic <u>spirit</u>. This fallen angelic beast will come upon the earth when he is released from the bottomless pit. The beast is the spirit of antichrist <u>that shall come</u>.

We see in Revelation chapter 9 that a star is given a key to the bottomless pit to open the pit. What does the word "STAR" in the book of Revelation symbolize?

Revelation 1:20 *"The mystery of the seven stars which thou sawest in my right hand, and the seven golden candlesticks. The <u>seven stars are the angels</u> of the seven churches…"*

In the book of Revelation the word STAR is symbolic of an <u>angel</u>.

Revelation 9:1 *And the fifth angel sounded, and I saw a **<u>star</u>** <u>fall</u> from heaven unto the earth: and to him was given the key of the bottomless pit.* ***2*** *And he opened the bottomless pit; and there arose a smoke out of the pit, as the smoke of a great furnace; and the sun and the air were darkened by reason of the smoke of the pit.* ***3*** *And there came out of the smoke locusts upon the earth: and unto them was given power, as the scorpions of the earth have power.*

This passage describes how the beast will be released out of the bottomless pit. In this vision, John saw a star fall from heaven. This star is a fallen <u>angel</u>, an angel that fell from heaven. This fallen angel is given a key to the <u>bottomless pit</u>.

Now do you think a fallen angel with a key to the bottomless pit is going to look at that key and say to himself, "No… that would be a bad thing to open that bottomless pit!"

No, the fallen angel will take that key and open the bottomless pit to release all the other fallen angels that are currently locked up in the bottomless pit. They will be released upon the earth. This will be the beginning of tribulation.

The angelic beast that ascends from the bottomless pit has a name.

Revelation 9:10 *And they had tails like unto scorpions, and there were stings in their tails: and their power was to hurt men five months. 11 And they had a king over them, which is the angel of the bottomless pit, whose name in the Hebrew tongue is Abaddon, but in the Greek tongue hath his name Apollyon.*

On the first day of tribulation as the bottomless pit is opened scorpion demons will be released from the pit with the power to hurt men for five months. The king of the scorpion demons is the angel of the bottomless pit. The angel who shall ascend out of the bottomless pit has the name Abaddon. In Greek his name is Apollyon.

Because of the importance of understanding the name of this fallen angel, the name is given in not just one, but two different languages. The name Apollyon means the Destroyer, or Destruction.

The four angelic beasts around the throne praise the Lord God Almighty, *"which was, and is and is to come..."* This phrase is in direct contrast to the description of the fallen angelic beast, Apollyon, who is described in the great mystery of Revelation 17:8 *"The beast that thou sawest was, and is not; and shall ascend out of the bottomless pit, and go into perdition:"*

"Holy, holy, holy, Lord God Almighty, which was, and is, and is to come." This phrase greatly glorifies and celebrates God.

The phrase is changed from a glorification of God to as a greatly deserved degradation applied to Apollyon the beast. This is seen in the great mystery of Revelation 17:8 *"The beast that thou sawest was, and is not; and shall ascend out of the bottomless pit, and go into perdition:"*

The beast was at the throne of God, but now is not, having been cast out of heaven. He shall ascend out of the bottomless pit. And ultimately go into perdition, as the beast Apollyon is cast into the lake of fire at the end of tribulation.

Consider again the contrast of these two phrases…

*Holy, Holy, Holy, Lord God Almighty, which **was, and is, and is to come**.*

*The beast that thou sawest **was, and is not**; and shall ascend out of the bottomless pit, and go into perdition:*

The purpose of this parallel phrase structure is to point out the beast's importance in the kingdom of darkness and to allude to Apollyon's failed attempt to take over God's throne in league with Satan. Apollyon is the only angel ever to be contrasted with God's attributes in such a direct and deserved degradation.

Chapter 3 Another Beast

The first beast ascends out of the bottomless pit. Is there a second beast? Is there another beast who ascends out of the earth?

Revelation 13:11 *And I beheld <u>another beast</u> coming up out of the earth; and he had two horns like a lamb, and he spake as a dragon.* **12** *And he <u>exerciseth all the power of the first beast</u> before him, and causeth the earth and them which dwell therein to worship the first beast...*

The second beast exercises all the power of the first beast. He can exercise the same power because he too is a fallen angelic beast.
Just like other angelic beasts this beast also has an amazing appearance as described in the scripture, *"he had two horns like a lamb, and he spake as a dragon."* Though the great supernatural power the second beast exercises, he causes those that dwell on the earth to worship the first beast.

Revelation 13:13 *And he doeth great wonders, so that he maketh <u>fire come down from heaven</u> on the earth in the sight of men,* **14** *And <u>deceiveth them that dwell</u> on the earth by the means of those miracles which he had power to do in the sight of the beast; saying to them that dwell on the earth, that they should make an image to the beast...*

Many years ago, a servant of God named Elijah called down fire from heaven. The ministry of Elijah was that of a <u>prophet</u>. The second beast calls down fire from heaven. The ministry of the second beast is that of a <u>prophet</u>.
Elijah was a good prophet. The second beast is a <u>false</u> prophet. **The second beast is the false prophet.**
The false prophet is not a man. The false prophet is a fallen angelic beast, an angel possessing great supernatural power. The false prophet is the second fallen angelic beast to ascend out of the bottomless pit. The

false prophet is a second fallen angelic beast who helps the first beast dominate the inhabitants of the earth.

Revelation 13:15 *And he had power to give life unto the image of the beast, that the image of the beast should both speak, and cause that as many as would not worship the image of the beast should be killed.* ***16*** *And he causeth* <u>*all, both small and great, rich and poor, free and bond*</u>*, to receive a mark in their right hand, or in their foreheads:* ***17*** *And that no man might buy or sell, save he that had the mark, or the name of the beast, or the number of his name.* ***18*** *Here is wisdom. Let him that hath understanding count the number of the beast: for it is the number of a man; and his number is Six hundred threescore and six.*

    The false prophet has the power to give <u>life</u> unto the image of the beast. As many as would not worship the image of the beast should be <u>killed</u>.
    This beast by great signs and wonders and by the threat of death causes mankind to worship the first beast. Scripture does not make mention of a single person other than the two witnesses who is able to stand up against the threat of the beast.
    He causeth <u>all</u> to receive a mark. He does not cause almost everyone or a majority of people to receive a mark. He causeth <u>all</u> to receive a mark. The use of the word <u>all</u> in the above scripture is also emphasized with the all encompassing language found in the passage. The description is not simply the term "all," but rather "*he causeth <u>all, both small and great, rich and poor, free and bond</u>, to receive a mark…*" No one is left out, no class of people can escape the mark.
    The mark is placed in the right hand, or on the <u>forehead</u>. The mark will be an indelible brand of the <u>name</u> of the beast Apollyon, or the <u>number</u> of his name. The number of his name is a number that symbolically means what his name means…DESTRUCTION. Those with the mark of the beast are <u>marked for destruction</u>.

Chapter 4 The Power of the Beast

Insight into the tremendous power of the beast is seen in the book of Isaiah. But to understand what Isaiah saw we must keep in mind several important details about each of the angelic beasts described in the book of Revelation.

The second beast to ascend out of the bottomless pit exercises all of the power of the first beast to ascend out of the bottomless pit. What power is this? Angelic beasts are angels of tremendous power. Their voices have the power to shake the doorposts in the temple of heaven. As we look in the book of Isaiah we must keep in mind the following details regarding the angelic beasts.

- The angelic beasts each have six wings.
- The angelic beasts cry, "HOLY, HOLY, HOLY…"
- The angelic beasts surround the throne of God in the temple in heaven, they are the closest angels to surround and to fly directly above the throne.

Isaiah saw the very same angels as described by John in Revelation 4:6-8. Isaiah's description of these angelic beasts or "seraphims" is seen in the following passage.

Isaiah 6:1 In the year that King Uzziah died I saw also the Lord sitting upon a throne, high and lifted up, and his train filled the temple. 2 Above it stood the seraphims: each one had <u>six wings</u>; with twain he covered his face, and with twain he covered his feet,, and with twain he did fly. 3 And one cried unto another, and said, <u>HOLY, HOLY, HOLY</u>, is the Lord of hosts: the whole earth is full of his glory. 4 And <u>the posts of the door moved</u> at the voice of him that cried, and the house was filled with smoke.

Isaiah did not see as John did that these angels had the appearance of beasts with the face of a lion, a calf, a man, and an eagle. When Isaiah saw these great angels with two wings they covered their faces, and with two wings they covered their feet, and with two wings they did fly. Therefore Isaiah did not see that their faces as they were covered with wings.

Note that each of these great angels has six wings and cries Holy, holy, holy…

The tremendous power of these angelic beasts or seraphim is describe in the phrase… "<u>And the posts of the door moved</u> at the voice of him that cried, and the house was filled with smoke."

Let's consider for a moment the tremendous power of the seraphims, the angelic beasts. If an angel appeared in a great cathedral on earth and cried, "Holy is the Lord," and the door posts of the cathedral shook and the house was filled with smoke we would be amazed at the power of such an angel. But we are talking about the temple of God in heaven! How powerful is an angel who can with his voice shake the doorposts of the temple of God in heaven?

Many mistakenly believe that those left behind after the rapture of the church will be able to refuse the mark of the beast. But consider for a moment if a human will be able to stand before the angel Apollyon the beast who had the power to shake the doorposts of heaven with his voice and who is backed by an army of scorpion demons and say, "Well, I just don't think I'll take that mark." No scripture is clear. ***Revelation 13:16*** *…he causeth **all**, both small and great, rich and poor, free and bond, to receive a mark…*

Jesus made it clear that escape through evacuation in the rapture is the only way of escape from the mark of the beast. *"Watch and pray always that ye may be accounted worthy to <u>escape</u> and to stand before the Son of man."* **Luke 21:36**

Those who criticize rapture theology say that it is merely "escape theology." They are actually criticizing Jesus theology. For Jesus taught of the importance of being ready to <u>escape</u> to stand before Him in the throne room in heaven.

The two fallen angelic beasts prior to the rebellion and their fall were not only very powerful but also very close to the throne in the temple of God in heaven. In rebellion, these two fallen angelic beasts attempted along with Satan to take over God's seat on the throne in the temple of God in heaven. In rebellion, these <u>angels of lawlessness</u> tried to <u>exalt themselves and take a seat on God's throne displaying themselves as being god</u>. This is the reason they were cast out of heaven. This is further detailed in chapter 7, Identity of the Man of Lawlessness.

The two evil angelic beasts are so bad and so <u>powerful</u> that when they were cast out of heaven the Lord had them locked up and concealed in the bottomless pit, a prison for fallen angels. They shall be released when the bottomless pit is opened on the day of the Lord as the punishment of tribulation begins. These two evil angelic beasts who shall come upon the earth are angels of great power. Previously, before their rebellion in heaven, they praised the Lord with cries of Holy, Holy, Holy. Their voices had the <u>power</u> to shake the doorposts of the temple of God in heaven.

Isaiah 6:3-8 *And one cried unto another, and said, HOLY, HOLY, HOLY, is the Lord of hosts: the whole earth is full of his glory. And the posts of the door moved at the voice of him that cried, and the house was filled with smoke. Then said I, Woe is me! For I am undone; because I am a man of unclean lips, and I dwell in the midst of a people of unclean lips: for mine eyes have seen the King, the Lord of hosts. Then flew one of the seraphims unto me, having a live coal in his hand, which he had taken with the tongs from off the altar: And <u>he laid it upon my mouth, and said, Lo, this hath touched thy lips; and thine iniquity is taken away, and thy sin purged</u>. Also I heard the voice of the Lord, saying, Whom shall I send, and who will go for us? Then said I, Here am I; send me.*

The faithful seraphim or angelic beast in the above passage has a unique ministry to Isaiah. This angelic beast touches Isaiah's lips with a live coal from the altar and in this way ministers grace and forgiveness to Isaiah in preparation for a special calling Isaiah is about to receive.

The angelic beast ministers a burning brand to Isaiah's lips to convey upon Isaiah grace and forgiveness. Consider for a moment the opposite brand the fallen angelic beast will minister to inhabitants of the earth.

Instead of ministering a burning mark of grace and forgiveness, the fallen angelic beast will administer a brand, the mark of the beast. This burning brand will be a mark of eternal unforgiveness and damnation.

After Isaiah's sin has been purged, the Lord asks, "Who shall I send, and who will go for us?" Isaiah answers, "Here am I, send me."

In a later chapter entitled "Strong Delusion" we shall see the answers to the following questions:

1. What is the Lord sending Isaiah to do?
2. Why is the Lord sending Isaiah to do it?

Chapter 5 The Mark of the Beast 666

Revelation 13:18 Here is wisdom. Let him that hath understanding count the number of the beast: for it is the number of a man; and his number is Six hundred threescore and six.

Revelation 13:16 And he causeth <u>all</u>, both small and great, rich and poor, free and bond, to receive a mark in their right hand, or in their foreheads: 17 And that no man might buy or sell, save he that had the mark, or <u>the name of the beast</u>, or <u>the number of his name</u>.

The mark of the beast will be the name of the beast or the number of his name. The number of his name is a number that means symbolically what his name means.

The name of the beast is Apollyon. That name means "<u>destruction</u>." Those with the mark of the beast are marked for <u>destruction</u>.

Who can best understand the mark of the beast? My good friend Glenn Smith the cowboy preacher will know this. <u>Cowboys</u> can best understand the mark of the beast. The mark is like a <u>brand</u> for branding cattle. The mark is a permanent designation of ownership. Those with the mark of the beast belong to the beast. Receiving the mark of the beast will be a painful involuntary event.

The beast shall with his great power <u>cause</u> or force a percentage of the population left behind after the rapture of the church to take his mark.

What is that percentage? What does scripture say?

Revelation 13:16 And he causeth <u>all</u>, both small and great, rich and poor, free and bond, to receive a mark...

What percentage is <u>all</u>? 100% of the earth's population shall be forced take the mark. This is why Jesus said that "as a snare" shall that day come upon "<u>all</u> them that dwell on the face of the entire earth."

Luke 21:35 *For as a snare shall it come on <u>all them that dwell</u> on the face of the whole earth.*

The mark of the beast will be a burning brand violently and forcefully placed on the hand or forehead. It is a permanent designation of ownership. Those who receive the mark of the beast are eternally lost, it is a mark of eternal destruction.

The mark of the beast is the name of the beast, or the number of his name. The name of the beast is <u>Apollyon</u>. The name Apollyon means <u>destruction</u>.

Those with the mark of the beast are marked for <u>destruction</u>. The mark of the beast is the name of the beast or <u>the number of his name</u>. The number of his name is the number that means what his name means. The number of his name is 666. That number is symbolic of the word <u>destruction</u>. The details of this symbolism are noted in the chapter which follows.

The mark of the beast is not a hidden computer chip. The mark of the beast is a brand, a mark for all to see and know who owns that person. Those with the mark of the beast will have the name <u>Apollyon</u> burned into their hand or forehead, or else the number symbolic of his name which is 666.

Those left behind shall be forced to take the mark of the beast. Interestingly, the elect shall also receive a mark but this will be a different mark. The elect shall escape the mark of the beast and they shall receive a different mark, the <u>mark of the Lord</u>.

Ultimately, all the servants of the Lord shall be given the <u>mark of the Lord</u> on their foreheads. This mark of the servants of the Lord shall be the <u>name of the Lord</u> written on their forehead.

Revelation 22:3 *And there shall be no more curse: but the throne of God and of the Lamb shall be in it; and his servants shall serve him:* ***4*** *And they shall see his face; and <u>his name shall be in their foreheads</u>.*

Review of certain events of the day of the Lord.

- The bottomless pit shall be opened.
- Jesus Christ shall be seen coming on the clouds in power and glory.
- Jesus shall send his angels to gather the elect and evacuate them to heaven to stand before the Lord at the throne.
- 144,000 of the children of Israel shall flee Jerusalem to the mount of Olives. They shall experience a visitation from the Lord Jesus Christ on the mount of Olives and they shall receive a seal of God's protection.

The 144,000 shall be sealed with the seal of God placed in their foreheads. This seal shall be the name of the Lord. They will then be taken to a place in the wilderness to be nourished there and protected for the entirety of the 3 and ½ year tribulation period. This seal will provide protection from the hoard of Apollyon's scorpion demons as seen in the following passage.

Revelation 9:1 *And the fifth angel sounded, and I saw a star fall from heaven unto the earth: and to him was given the key of the bottomless pit. **2** And he opened the bottomless pit; and there arose a smoke out of the pit, as the smoke of a great furnace; and the sun and the air were darkened by reason of the smoke of the pit. **3** And there came out of the smoke locusts upon the earth: and unto them was given power, as the scorpions of the earth have power. **4** And it was commanded them that they should not hurt the grass of the earth, neither any green thing, neither any tree; <u>but only those men which have not the seal of God in their foreheads</u>. **5** And to them it was given that they should not kill them, but that they should be tormented five months: and their torment was as the torment of a scorpion, when he striketh a man. **6** And in those days shall men seek death, and shall not find it; and shall desire to die, and death shall flee from them.*

When will the 144,000 of the children of Israel receive this mark of the Lord which shall protect them?

***Revelation 7:2** And I saw another angel ascending from the east, having the seal of the living God: and he cried with a loud voice to the <u>four angels</u>, to whom it was given to hurt the earth and the sea, **3** Saying, Hurt not the earth, neither the sea, nor the trees<u>, till we have sealed the servants of our God in their foreheads</u>. **4** And I heard the number of them which were sealed: and there were sealed an <u>hundred and forty and four thousand</u> of all the tribes of the children of Israel.*

Note in the above passage the mystery of four angels given to hurt the earth. These four angels are not allowed to hurt the earth until later after the 144,000 receive the seal of God's protection. This sealing of the 144,000 is also seen a in yet another vision of this same event in a later chapter of the book of Revelation.

***Revelation 14:1** And I looked, and, lo, a Lamb stood on the mount Sion, and with him an <u>hundred forty and four thousand, having his Father's name written in their foreheads</u>.*

In summary, both the elect and the lost shall receive a mark. It will either be the mark of the beast, or the mark of the Lord. For the elect, the mark of the Lord will be the name of the Lord. For the lost, the mark of the beast will be the name of the beast which is Apollyon or Destruction. Those with the mark of the beast are marked for DESTRUCTION.

The 144,000 of the children of Israel shall have a mark, the name of the Lord, in their forehead. The raptured church shall also have a mark, the mark of the Lord. This will be the name of the Lord written in their foreheads as seen in the following scripture.

***Revelation 22:3** And there shall be no more curse: but the throne of God and of the Lamb shall be in it; and his servants shall serve him: **4** And they shall see his face; and <u>his name shall be in their foreheads</u>.*

Chapter 6 Here is wisdom - Understanding 666

***Revelation 13:16** And he causeth <u>all</u>, both small and great, rich and poor, free and bond, to receive a mark in their right hand, or in their foreheads: **17** And that no man might buy or sell, save he that had <u>the mark</u>, or <u>the name of the beast</u>, or <u>the number of his name</u>. **18** Here is wisdom. Let him that hath understanding count the number of the beast: for it is the number of a man; and his number is Six hundred threescore and six.*

This chapter is the transcript of a sermon presented by the author on November 29, 2001 at the fifth of a series of meetings entitled "The Kingdom of Heaven Revival."

"Now… in verse 16… and we need to skip a little bit cause it's hard to teach the whole book in one night, but we're trying…

***Revelation 13:16** And he causeth all, both small and great, rich and poor, free and bond, to receive a mark in their right hand, or in their foreheads: **17** And that no man might buy or sell, save he that had ...*

- ONE OF THESE THINGS…
- THE MARK which is
- THE NAME of the beast, or
- THE NUMBER OF HIS NAME.

We know what the name of this beast is. Because it tells us that in Revelation chapter 9. The name of the beast is Apollyon. And that name means destruction, so his name actually is DESTRUCTION.

So the mark of the beast is the name of the beast or the number of his name. The number of his name is the number that means symbolically what his name means.

What is that number. Well it tells us, it is 6. It is 666.

It tells us... *"here is wisdom. Let him that hath understanding count the number of the beast:"*

Let him who has understanding count...I mentioned E.W. Bullinger in his book *Numbers in Scripture*. He said that counting the number of the beast has to do with calculating the number. Numbers have symbolic meaning, and it is more that just the counting up of the gamatria of a name.

It means more than that. The number has to have a symbolic meaning. It is figuring out what the symbolic meaning of the number is. And when the symbolic meaning of that number matches the meaning of the name itself, then that's it. That is the answer.

Some numbers have symbolic meaning in scripture. That's what E.W. Bullinger's book teaches in detail.

O.K. The number of his name is 6, it's 666. The number 6 is also the number of man.

Now, has anybody studied the symbolic or prophetic meaning of numbers?

- What is the number of witness? Two.
- Why, because *"out of the mouth of two or three witnesses are all things established."* This is in multiple scriptures.
- What is the number of perfect witness. THREE.
- Yes, and remember this. 3 is the number of perfect witness.
- What is the number of grace? Five. Right, very good.
- What is the number of perfection or completion? Seven.
- What is the number of new beginnings? Eight. Why?
- Because there were 8 souls on the ark.
- So the number 8 is symbolic of new beginnings.
- What is the number of man? Six. Right.
- The number of man is six, because man was created on the sixth day. Six is symbolic of man especially meaning as being separate from God which is a state that leads to what? Destruction.

Now the scripture says, *"Let him that hath understanding count the number of the beast: for it is the number of a man;..."* **Revelation 13:18**

Note this does not mean that the number 6 is that of an individual human or of <u>a man</u>.

The King James version translated the Greek word at that point as <u>of a man</u>. But if you look at that exact same Greek word in other areas of scripture, it can also be translated as just "<u>of man</u>," as in mankind or man in general. An example of this is 2 Peter 1:21 *"For the prophecy came not in old time by the will <u>of man</u>:.."* It is the same Greek word.

So it could also just as well have been translated...*Let him that has understanding, count the number of the beast: for it is the number <u>of man</u>.* The number of man is six, this is because man was created on the sixth day of the week during creation. But six also has another symbolic meaning in scripture which fits symbolically and matches the name of the beast as shall see.

E.W. Bullinger also says that the repetitive nature of <u>repeating the number</u> three times gives you the concentrated essence of the meaning of the number. In other words, if 6 is a bad number, then 666 is really bad. We may mention that again in a minute. But let's just review a minute...

Verse 17 *And that no man might buy or sell, save he that had...*
- THE MARK or
- THE NAME or
- THE NUMBER OF THE NAME ... Which is 6.

So the next step is to find in scripture if the number 6 means the same thing that his name means, which is DESTRUCTION. Then those puzzle pieces fit together and our mystery is solved.

See this puzzle much like a picture puzzle has interlocking pieces which not only have to fit this way, but it has to fit that way. And if the number 6 means destroyer or destruction, then our mystery is solved because the beast's name is DESTRUCTION which in Greek translates as APOLLYON.

Well, let's look and see. Now God is going to destroy the destroyer. Like it says in Revelation chapter 11, but the earth is also going to be destroyed in the future. But the earth was previously destroyed once in the past. And it was destroyed by water, by a flood. Guess what chapter of Genesis the destroying of the earth was in? The answer is 6.

Chapter six. So let's turn there. And we will see the same thing in Exodus 14. In Genesis chapter six, we will see a pattern indicating that the number six or 600 means DESTRUCTION.

Genesis 6 verse 7 the Lord says, *"I will <u>destroy</u> man whom I have created from the face of the earth; both man, and beast..."*

And he repeats this in verse 17, *"And, behold, I, even I, do bring a flood of waters upon the earth, to <u>destroy</u> all flesh,..."*

And again a third time in chapter 7 he says, *"...and every living substance that I have made will I <u>destroy</u> from off the face of the earth."*

And in verse <u>6</u>, how old was Noah when the flood came to bring destruction of all the evil on earth? Can anyone guess? Let me give you a hint. Noah was not 599 years old when the destruction came, and he was not 601 years old when the destruction came. He was exactly 600 years old. So when Noah turned 600 it was a sign that destruction was coming. 600 is a sign of coming destruction.

And in verse 11, it repeats this... *"in the **<u>six</u>** hundreth year of Noah's life the earth was **<u>destroyed</u>**."*

But there is more. Let's turn to Exodus chapter 14. Pharaoh had let the children of Israel go out of captivity. But Pharaoh's heart was hardened and in verse 5 he says, *"Why have we done this, that we have let Israel go from serving us?"*

Pharaoh then made ready his chariot, and took his people with him: They went out to destroy Israel at the red sea. Pharaoh sent a number of chosen chariots to bring destruction to Israel. How many chariots did Pharaoh send? Let me give you another hint. Pharaoh did not send 599 chariots to bring destruction of Israel, and he did not send 601 chariots to bring destruction. He sent exactly 600 chariots because 600 is the number symbolic of coming destruction.

Six hundred chosen chariots sent to bring destruction to Israel. And what happened to this destroyer? He was destroyed. And how did he get destroyed? The destroyer of Israel was cast into the red sea. And the red sea is a picture of what? The lake of fire. And the beast Apollyon, <u>the DESTROYER</u>, is going to be destroyed by being cast into a lake of fire.

The mark of the beast is the number of his name. His name is Apollyon which means destruction, the number of his name is 6, because 6 means destruction. And 666 is the concentrated essence of destruction. Having 6 three times combines two symbolic numbers.

The number <u>3</u> is the number of <u>perfect witness</u>, and 6 means destruction. 666 *(6 associated with 3) or three sixes* is the <u>perfect witness of destruction</u>.

To review, the mark the beast is the name of the beast Apollyon which means destruction, or else the mark is the number of his name which is 666. The number of his name is the number which symbolically means what his name means. That meaning is destruction. And the number 6 is symbolic of destruction in scripture. Those with the mark of the beast are marked for destruction.

APOLLYON, APOLLYON, APOLLYON

DESTRUCTION, DESTRUCTION, DESTRUCTION

666

3 sixes
The perfect witness of DESTRUCTION

Chapter 7 Identity of the Man of Lawlessness

*2 **Thessalonians 2:1** Now we beseech you, brethren, by the coming of our Lord Jesus Christ, and by <u>our gathering together unto him</u>, **2** That ye be not soon shaken in mind, or be troubled, neither by spirit, nor by word, nor by letter as from us, as that the day of Christ is at hand. **3** Let no man deceive you by any means: for that day shall not come, except there come a falling away first, and that man of sin be revealed, the son of perdition; **4** Who opposeth and exalteth himself above all that is called God, or that is worshipped; so that he as God sitteth in the temple of God, shewing himself that he is God. **5** Remember ye not, that, when I was yet with you, I told you these things? **6** And now ye know what withholdeth that he might be <u>revealed in his time</u>. **7** For the mystery of iniquity doth already work: only he who now letteth will let, until he be taken out of the way. **8** And then shall that Wicked be revealed, whom the Lord shall consume with the spirit of his mouth, and shall destroy with the brightness of his coming: **9** Even him, whose coming is after the working of Satan with all power and signs and lying wonders, **10** And with all deceivableness of unrighteousness in them that perish; because they received not the love of the truth, that they might be saved. **11** And for this cause God shall send them <u>strong delusion</u>, that they should believe a lie: **12** That they all might be damned who believed not the truth, but had pleasure in unrighteousness.*

Verse 1 speaks of the coming of our Lord Jesus Christ and the rapture of the Church, *"<u>our gathering together unto him</u>."*

The next verse speaks of the day of the Lord, *"day of Christ."* This is the day that we shall be <u>gathered together unto him.</u> The rapture of the Church shall occur on the day of Christ, <u>the day of the Lord</u>. Following this is the admonition not to be shaken or troubled that the day of the Lord is at hand. Instead of the phrase "<u>at hand</u>, the NASB translates the passage as "**<u>has come</u>**."

Whichever translation is better is not as important as the knowledge that <u>the day of the Lord</u> has not yet come else we would know it for sure as verse 3 shall demonstrate. In verse 3 we learn that when the day of the Lord has arrived the man of lawlessness shall no longer be concealed. We also learn that an event known as the <u>apostasy</u> or <u>falling away</u> shall occur first, and only then shall the man of lawlessness be revealed.

The man of lawlessness is also known as the son of <u>destruction</u> (NASB) or son of perdition. (KJV)

2 Thessalonians 2:2&3 That you be not soon shaken in mind, or be troubled, neither by spirit, nor by word nor by letter as from us, as that the day of Christ is at hand. Let no man deceive you by any means: for that day shall not come, except their come a <u>falling away</u> first, and that man of sin be revealed, the son of perdition;

The Greek word translated as <u>falling away</u> is the word "apostasia" Stongs #646. The word is translated "apostasy" in the NASB and means <u>defection</u> as in "a defection from truth, or leaving the truth behind" and literally means to <u>forsake</u>.

According to the Random House Dictionary sited at Dictionary.com the definition of the word <u>forsake</u> is…

to quit or leave entirely; abandon; desert: <u>She has forsaken her country for an island in the South Pacific</u>.

In the event of the rapture of the Church, the elect shall leave entirely, abandon and desert the earth. <u>The Church shall have forsaken the earth for the throne room of heaven to stand before the Son of man</u>.

This defection or <u>rapture</u> of the church must come <u>first</u> before the man of lawlessness can be revealed because it is the church that <u>restrains</u> or withholds the man of lawlessness from being revealed.

2 Thessalonians 2:6 And now ye know what <u>withholdeth</u> that he might be <u>revealed in his time</u>. 7 For the mystery of iniquity doth already work: only he who now letteth will let<u>, until he be taken out of the way</u>. 8 And then shall that Wicked <u>be revealed</u>, whom the Lord shall consume *with the spirit of his mouth, and shall destroy with the brightness of his coming:*

The KJV is slightly different from the NASB which states in verse 6 *"you know what restrains him now."* And in verse 7, *"<u>he who now restrains will do so until he is taken out of the way.</u>"*

Who is the man of lawlessness? What is his identity? First we must ask… What is a man? I will give you a hint, there are two possibilities. Consider the following two scriptures.

__1 Corinthians 15:45__ And so it is written, The first man Adam was made a living soul;

Is the man of lawlessness a human being, a descendant of Adam? Is there another possible answer? There is a clue to the mystery of the <u>man</u> of lawlessness found in Daniel.

__Daniel 9:21__ Yea, whiles I was speaking in prayer, even the __<u>man</u> <u>Gabriel</u>__, whom I had seen in the vision at the beginning, being caused to fly swiftly, touched me about the time of the evening oblation.

In this case, the angel Gabriel is called a <u>man</u>. Angels are also called men in Genesis 18:2. It is therefore possible that a <u>fallen angel</u> could also be called a <u>man</u>.

Is the man of lawlessness an angel, or a man who is a descendent of Adam? There is a clue in the following Scripture …

2 Thessalonians 2:6-8 *NASB*
And you know what restrains him <u>now</u>…

Paul wrote, *"and you know what restrains him <u>now</u>…"* If the man of lawlessness were a mortal man who was being restrained <u>at that time</u> then he would be dead by now. And, we know that the fallen angel

Apollyon is now being restrained in the bottomless pit and will be revealed at the time ordained.

2 Thessalonians 2:3 *NASB Let no one in any way deceive you, for it will not come unless the apostasy comes first, and the man of lawlessness is revealed, the son of <u>destruction</u>.*

- The Greek word translated as "destruction" is <u>Apoleia</u>.
- The name of the beast is <u>Apollyon</u>.

The man of lawlessness is the beast, the fallen the angel Apollyon. But what about the next verse, verse 4?

2 Thessalonians 2:4 *NASB Who opposes and exalts himself above every so-called god or object of worship, so that he takes his seat in the temple of God, displaying himself as being God.*

It has commonly been thought that the temple must be rebuilt on earth for this scripture to be fulfilled. But actually, the scripture was previously fulfilled at the throne in the temple of God in Heaven. Apollyon and Satan fell in rebellion when they tried to take over God's throne in the temple in Heaven. The <u>temple of God</u> in Heaven is the temple that Apollyon <u>took a seat in declaring himself as being God</u>. This was the fulfillment of 2 Thessalonisians 2:4. For this cause was the beast Apollyon, the man of lawlessness, cast out of heaven. This is why the beast is called the man of lawlessness, and that is why he is now restrained in the bottomless pit.

Chapter 8 Strong Delusion

Isaiah 55:6 *Seek ye the Lord while he may be found.*

Isaiah knew that a day was coming in the future when men would no longer be able to seek and find the Lord.

2 Thessalonians 2:2-12 *That you be not soon shaken in mind, or be troubled, neither by spirit, nor by word nor by letter as from us, as that the day of Christ is at hand. Let no man deceive you by any means: for that day shall not come, except their come a falling away first, and that man of sin be revealed, the son of perdition; Who opposeth and exalteth himself above all that is called God, or that is worshipped; so that he as God sitteth in the temple of God, shewing himself that he is God. Remember ye not, that, when I was with you, I told you these things? And now ye know what withholdth that he might be revealed in his time. For the mystery of iniquity doth already work; only he who now letteth will let, until he be taken out of the way. And then shall that Wicked be revealed, whom the Lord shall consume with the spirit of his mouth, and shall destroy with the brightness of his coming: Even him, whose coming is after the working of Satan with all power and signs and lying wonders, And with all deceivableness of unrighteousness in them that perish; because they received not the love of the truth, that they might be saved. And for this cause God shall send them <u>strong delusion</u>, that they should believe a lie: That they all might be damned who believed not the truth, but had pleasure in unrighteousness.*

After the rapture of the church the man of lawlessness, the beast Apollyon shall be revealed as he ascends out of the bottomless pit. Those who are left behind on the earth will fall to the deception of the beast because they received not the love of the truth, that they might be saved. *And for this cause God shall send them strong delusion, that they should believe a lie: That they all might be damned who believed not the truth, but had pleasure in unrighteousness.*

Remember in Isaiah chapter 6, Isaiah saw the Lord in the temple in heaven and also he saw the seraphims, the angelic beasts. One of the seraphims or angelic beasts touches Isaiah's lips with a coal and purges Isaiah's sins.

Isaiah 6:6-8 *Then flew one of the seraphims unto me, having a live coal in his hand, which he had taken with the tongs from off the altar: And he laid it upon my mouth, and said, Lo, this hath touched thy lips; and thine iniquity is taken away, and thy sin purged. Also I heard the voice of the Lord, saying, Whom shall I send, and who will go for us? Then said I, Here am I; send me.*

Isaiah will be sent back to earth for a special prophetic mission. This mission is to prophesy strong delusion upon a people who would one day worship the fallen angelic beast during the tribulation period.

Isaiah 6:8–11 *...Then said I, Here am I, send me. And he said, Go, and tell this people, Hear ye indeed, but understand not; and see ye indeed, but perceive not. Make the heart of this people fat, and make their ears heavy, and shut their eyes; lest they see with their eyes, and hear with their ears, and understand with their heart, and convert, and be healed. Then said I, Lord, how long?*

Isaiah asked the obvious question. Isaiah must prophesy over a people strong delusion that keeps that people from turning to the Lord, a strong delusion that keeps a people away from conversion and salvation. The obvious question to Isaiah is, *"Lord, how long?"* When can this strong delusion be reversed? The Lord answers...

Isaiah 6:11 *Then said I, Lord, how long? And he answered, Until the cities be wasted without inhabitant, and houses without man, and the land be utterly desolate,*

Strong delusion will be upon those left on earth as they all worship the beast and take his mark. Strong delusion will remain upon them all until they are all dead. Only the nation of Israel will be left on the earth as they are taken to a special place prepared by God, marked in their foreheads with a mark of protection, and nourished by God in the wilderness for the entire 3 & ½ year tribulation period.

In the next verse the Lord mentions the rapture of the church, which is the Lord's evacuation of the body of Christ escaping the earth as tribulation begins. In the rapture the Lord removes the church to heaven, a far away place, as the church forsakes or leaves the earth.

***Isaiah 6:11-12** Then said I, Lord, how long? And he answered, Until the cities be wasted without inhabitant, and houses without man, and the land be utterly desolate, And the Lord have removed men far away, and there be a great forsaking in the midst of the land.*

In the rapture those in Christ shall forsake the earth as the Lord removes men far away to the throne room in heaven. Those left behind shall be destroyed as they shall be under strong delusion… *"Until the cities be wasted without inhabitant, and houses without man, and the land be utterly desolate."* Is there other evidence in scripture that those "left behind" after the rapture will all be destroyed? Jesus teaches us what will happen on his day, the day of the Lord.

***Luke 17:24** For as lightning, that lighteneth out of the one part under heaven, shineth unto the other part under heaven; so shall also the Son of man be in his day.*

His day is the day of the LORD. Just as it takes but a moment for lightning to flash across the sky, the day of the LORD will suddenly and unexpectedly come upon the earth.

***Luke 17:26** And as it was in the days of Noe so shall it be also in the days of the Son of man. They did eat, they drank, they married wives,* *they were given in marriage, until the day that Noe entered into the ark, and the flood came, and destroyed them all. Likewise also as it was in the days of Lot; they did eat, they drank, they bought, they sold, they planted, they builded; But the same day that Lot went out of Sodom it rained fire and brimstone from heaven, and <u>destroyed them all</u>. Even thus shall it be in the day when the Son of man is revealed.*

THE DAY OF THE LORD will come upon the earth just like an iceberg came upon the Titanic. The rapture of the church is like the last lifeboat to escape the sinking ship. All who are left behind will be marked for destruction. As it was in the days of Noah, and as it was in the days of Lot after evacuation took place, <u>all</u> who were 'Left Behind' were destroyed. After the righteous were evacuated ALL wickedness was thoroughly cleansed by total destruction of all who were <u>left behind</u>.

In the last verses of Isaiah chapter 6 the Lord reveals a word picture of the final events and the final result of these end time events. The accurate interpretation of this verse is a mystery for it is a word picture only understood when seen in context with the events of the entire chapter.

Before we look at theses scripture they will be explained. In verse 13 the Lord shows a picture of Israel, the Lord's nation, remaining on the earth. The Lord's portion is "a tenth" and Israel remaining on the earth being protected and nourished by God during the tribulation represents that tenth described by the phrase, "But yet in it shall be a tenth." The return of the Church back to earth, which had previously been removed far away, is described with the next brief phrase, "and it shall return."

The next phrase, "and shall be eaten," describes the Lord enjoying the fruit of his mighty works and his enjoyment of having his people with him on the earth cleansed from all wickedness. The verse ends with the word picture of a tree. This is a tree with the substance of life remaining in it after all leaves have been cast off. In this same way, the earth after all the wicked are cast off, will have remaining in it the substance of life consisting only of the children of God or "holy seed."

As a final result of the events of Isaiah chapter 6, only the holy seed will be the entire substance of life on earth.

***Isaiah 6:11-13** Then said I, Lord, how long? And he answered, Until the cities be wasted without inhabitant, and the houses without man, and the land be utterly desolate, And the Lord have removed men far away, and there be a great forsaking in the midst of the land. But yet in it shall be a tenth, and it shall return, and shall be eaten: as a teil tree, and as an oak, whose substance is in them, when they cast their leaves: so the holy seed shall be the substance thereof.*

Chapter 9 Star of Wonder

Star of wonder, star of night! Star of royal beauty bright; westward leading, still proceeding, guide us to thy Perfect Light.
Excerpted from the Christmas carol, "We Three Kings of Orient Are" (John Henry Hopkins, 1857)

Matthew 2:1 *Now when Jesus was born in Bethlehem of Judaea in the days of Herod the king, behold, there came wise men from the east to Jerusalem,* **2** *Saying, Where is he that is born King of the Jews? for we have seen his <u>star</u> in the east, and are come to worship him.*

Matthew 2:10 *When they saw the <u>star</u>, they rejoiced with exceeding great joy.* **11** *And when they were come into the house, they saw the young child with Mary his mother, and fell down, and worshipped him: and when they had opened their treasures, they presented unto him gifts; gold, and frankincense, and myrrh.*

The wise men rejoiced with exceeding great joy when they saw the star. They knew they would soon stand before the King of Kings. Why did they believe this? What characteristics of the star made the wise men believe that the King of Kings had been born?

The DVD video <u>The Star of Bethlehem</u> by Frederick Larson details the possible symbolic significance the wise men may have perceived leading to their quest to worship the King of Kings. Larson explains this in a very interesting way. He used a computer program that shows the present location of all the stars and planets. But this program also can be run backwards to see the position of the stars yesterday, last year, or even 2000 years ago.

According to Larson in 3 B.C. the planet Jupiter, symbolically known as the <u>king</u> planet, closely passed or made conjunction with the star Regulus which is known as the <u>king</u> star. The name Regulus is derived from the same root word from which we get the term "regal."

But Jupiter did not merely pass Regulus once but tightly made a circle passing a second time. Amazingly, Jupiter then made another tight circle in a phenomenon of retrograde motion and passed Regulus a third time. The king planet had formed a halo or crown above the king star. This event was symbolic of a recognition of the King of Kings and may have been seen near the time of the conception of Jesus that took place within the virgin Mary by a miracle of the Holy Spirit.

Note that the king planet passed the king star three times. The reader of this book will recall as we studied in an earlier chapter that the number three is the number of perfect witness. We studied, for example, that three sixes 666 is the perfect witness of Destruction which defines the mark of the beast.

The phenomenon of the king planet Jupiter passing the king star Regulus three times has symbolic significance. This may have been considered by the wise men to be a perfect witness of the coming of the King of Kings.

The wise men would have continued to observe Jupiter the king planet very closely. Nine months later the king planet Jupiter came into a tight conjunction with Venus, the mother planet, forming the brightest star ever seen by the wise men. The king now had a mother. The King of Kings was born! The wise men gathered their gifts of gold, frankincense, and myrrh. They saddled their camels and were off to seek and worship the King of Kings.

But as interesting as the Star of Bethlehem phenomenon was, an even more dramatic sign was seen this decade in the heavens indicating the imminent return of the King of Kings. Acts chapter two prophesied a wonder in heaven that would indicate the imminent return of Jesus Christ. This modern star of wonder would precede and portend the great and notable day of the Lord in Acts 2:20.

Acts 2:19&20 And I will shew wonders in heaven above, and signs in the earth…
…Before that great and notable day of the Lord.

The following quotation is from the website of the International Journal of High Energy Physics...

http://cerncourier.com/cws/article/cern/28863

Cited as Further Reading

D W Fox *et al.* 2003 *Nature* **422** 284

"In January 2002, the supergiant star V838 Monocerotis, located about 20,000 light-years away in the constellation Monoceros (the Unicorn), suddenly became 600,000 times more luminous than the Sun. This made it temporarily the brightest star in our galaxy. The light from this dramatic eruption created a unique phenomenon known as a "light echo" when it reflected off dust shells around the red star at the centre. This sequence of pictures from the NASA/ESA Hubble Space Telescope's Advanced Camera for Surveys, obtained between May and December 2002, shows apparent changes in the appearance of the circumstellar dust as different parts are illuminated sequentially. From the first to last image, the apparent diameter of the nebula appears to balloon from four to seven light-years. This creates the illusion that the dust is expanding into space faster than the speed of light. In reality the dust shells are not expanding at all, but it is simply the light from the stellar flash that is sweeping out into the nebula. (NASA, European Space Agency and H E Bond (STScI).)"

The above article was published after the light echo had reached a diameter of seven light-years. Just one year and two months later, the diameter of the light echo ballooned an additional 6.6 light-years to reach a diameter of 13.6 light-years as documented in the Hubble Telescope photograph on the front cover. Photographs of the earlier expansion are on the back cover. The light echo continues to sweep out through the nebula at a steady velocity of approximately 3 light-years per year.

Mysteries remain regarding the supergiant star V838 Monocerotis. One mystery is the following question regarding the explanation given in the article by D.W. Fox et al. For the dust to be expanding into space faster than the speed of light would indeed be impossible. The explanation given is that the dust is not expanding at all, but "simply" being illuminated from the stellar flash sweeping out into the nebula. But the ultimate solution to this mystery is not so simple. For how can light from the stellar flash sweep out to bring illumination covering a vast distance in space at a rate faster than the speed of light? It is just as impossible for light to move faster than the speed of light as it is for dust to expand faster than the speed of light.

On the 6th day of the year 2002 the supergiant star Monocerotis suddenly pulsed a great light making it the brightest star in our galaxy. How bright was this massive pulse of light from Monocerotis? Was there a symbolic prophetic significance to this amazing event? Let me give you a hint to this mystery in the form of a riddle. Noah was not a mere 599 years old but he was 600 years old when the destruction of the flood came. Pharaoh did not send a mere 599 chariots but rather he sent 600 chariots to bring destruction to Israel at the Red Sea. If the stellar flash of Monocerotis were a sign of coming destruction exactly how bright would it be? This is the solution to that mystery. The amazing light of Monocerotis was not a mere 599,000 times the brightness of the sun but was exactly 600,000 brighter than the sun. Does the reader remember the symbolic significance of the number 600?

Six hundred is the number symbolic of coming destruction. Could the great light from Monocerotis be a sign? What do you think?

It is a sign. And yet another clue of symbolism in this great mystery involves the incredible speed of the expansion of the light and dust cloud surrounding this modern star of wonder.

The photograph gracing the cover of this book is the supergiant star V838 Monocerotis as imaged by the Hubble Space Telescope February 8, 2004. On the back cover are a series of photographs showing the rapid expansion in size of this phenomenon.

This space phenomenon covers a distance of incomprehensible magnitude being 13.6 light-years wide. By comparison our own solar system would be an undetectable speck less than 1/500 of an inch in size if placed to size in the photograph on the cover of this book. For light to travel from our sun to the planet Pluto takes only about 5 and ½ hours. For light to travel from our sun to earth takes approximately 8.3 minutes.

For light to traverse the radius, from the center star to the edge, of this massive phenomenon in space would take 6.8 years. But amazingly light from this star of wonder has reached the edge in just slightly over 2 years.

How much faster than the known speed of light is this amazing light from Monocerotis traveling? From the central point of this star, which suddenly pulsed a great light in January 2002, to the edge of the dust cloud as recorded February 8, 2004, is a distance reported as 6.8 light-years (1/2 the diameter of 13.6 light-years.) The light from Monocerotis would have to travel at about 3X the known speed of light to reach the edge of the dust cloud in the time recorded of just slightly over 2 years. Star Trek fans will identify this velocity as WARP 3 which is 3X the speed of light. This speed appears impossible but is clearly documented in the time lapse Hubble Telescope photographs. But what of the symbolic prophetic significance of a light that moves <u>three</u> times the known speed of light? And how do scientists of astronomy attempt to describe the behavior of Monocerotis?

Scientific papers have attempted to offer a viable explanation of the behavior of V838 Monocerotis such as the following website article which has termed the behavior of this supergiant star as the "Born Again" phenomenon.

http://articles.adsabs.harvard.edu/full/2005MNRAS.361..695L

SAO/NASA Astrophysics Data System (ADS)

Title: A new model for V838 Monocerotis: a born-again object including an episode of accretion

Authors: Lawlor, T. M.

Journal: Monthly Notices of the Royal Astronomical Society, Volume 361, Issue 2, pp. 695-700.

Bibliographic Code: 2005MNRAS.361..695L

The astronomical term "born again" in the above article has no intended spiritual implications. But the "born again" terminology is ironic considering the prophetic and evangelistic implications of this star of wonder as a fulfillment of the prophecy of Acts 2:19.

The great stellar flash of supergiant star V838 Monocerotis is characterized by details of symbolic prophetic significance. In January 2002, just four months after the day the twin towers fell in 2001, this star of wonder suddenly became the brightest star in our galaxy and was reported to be <u>600</u>,000 times more brilliant than our sun. In an earlier chapter, we studied evidence that the number 600 is symbolic of coming <u>destruction</u>. The number 600,000 would be an even more emphatic symbol of coming destruction. And this would be an even more emphatic sign when associated with the number <u>three,</u> the number of <u>perfect witness</u>.

Monocerotis was reported to be 600,000 brighter than the sun. The velocity of this amazing light was recorded photographically to be traveling at around 3 times the speed of light.

600,000 is symbolic of <u>destruction</u> and 3 is symbolic of a <u>perfect witness</u>. Monocerotis is a fulfillment of Acts 2:19 as a wonder in heaven above and is a <u>perfect witness of coming destruction</u>. As a fulfillment of Acts 2:19 it is a sign that the day of the Lord noted in Acts 2:20 is about to take place. Soon we shall stand before the King of Kings.

Amazing as this is, there is more. In 2004 when I first saw the space photograph I was immediately drawn to it. I placed the photograph on the cover of a DVD video teaching series I released on the mysteries contained in the book of Revelation. Several weeks later as I viewed enlarged prints of the photograph some hidden images began to emerge. Much like hidden images in a child's picture puzzle, the images were initially undetectable but very apparent when finally noticed. Many of us have seen children's picture puzzles which could be the picture of a tree for example with instructions to find a cup, a spoon, a thimble, and a baseball bat hidden within the tree.

Amazingly, hidden within the space photograph were definite characteristics of images of the four angelic beasts surrounding the throne of God as described by John in Revelation 4:8. The characteristics of a lion, a longhorn steer, a man, and an eagle jump out at me every time I view the photograph. Other characteristics of angelic beasts are also present such as abundant wings that partially cover portions of their faces and feet much like Isaiah described these seraphims in Isaiah chapter 6. Details of these hidden images may be viewed online at the website www.biblemystery.com

On the back cover are photographs of the early expansion of the Monocerotis light echo starting May 2002. Amazingly, study of these photographs and a video montage available for review at my website reveal characteristics which Ezekiel reported as a <u>wheel within a wheel</u> and out of the midst the appearance of four beasts – a lion, a man, a calf, and an eagle. This video montage and further study of the photographs are available to study free online at www.biblemystery.com which also has links to the Hubble Space Telescope website.

The prophetic message conveyed by this modern star of wonder is brief and clear…

Destruction is coming.
Repent, for the Kingdom of Heaven is at Hand.
Seek ye the Lord while he may be found.

For the wise who have received Jesus Christ as Lord this modern star of wonder is a source of exceeding great joy. Is it a sign that we shall soon stand before the King of Kings. It is a sign.

Matthew 2:10 *When they saw the star, they rejoiced with exceeding great joy.*

Recommended study…The Star of Bethlehem DVD video by Frederick A. Larson available at www.bethlehemstar.net

This excellent presentation from a biblical and scientific perspective gives deep insight into the star of Bethlehem phenomenon. Elements of astronomical symbolism relating to this phenomenon are presented in a scholarly method with dramatic impact. These signs of astronomical symbolism may have been perceived by the wise men triggering their pursuit to worship the King of Kings with gifts of gold, frankincense, and myrrh.

A point to ponder… The name of the <u>king star</u> Regulus was a key to the prophetic symbolism the wise men likely saw in the star of Bethlehem. Does the name of the star Monocerotis convey a symbolic prophetic mystery? The following is a hint for those who like riddles.
- Regulus is the <u>king</u> star. Monocerotis is the _____ star.
- Regulus announced the birth of the King.
- Monocerotis reveals the coming destruction of the _____.

The star Monocerotis is the namesake of the constellation Monoceros in which it is located. The modern interpretation of the name Monoceros is "unicorn." However, the name "monoceros" can also refer to a far older mythological fierce <u>beast</u>, who is part lion and also partly made up of other creatures. This beast, the monoceros, was depicted in Assyrian art around the third millenium B.C. The name Monoceros and Monocerotis share this same ancient meaning - a fierce <u>beast</u> who is part lion and also made up of other creatures. These definitions are referenced at the website of the Chandra Spacecraft X-Ray Observatory and the Harvard-Smithsonian Center for Astrophysics as follows… http://chandra.harvard.edu/photo/constellations/monoceros.html

Monocerotis is the <u>beast star</u> and is located in the <u>beast constellation</u> Monoceros. Early this decade the beast star suddenly became the brightest star in our galaxy, 600,000 the brilliance of the sun, a number symbolic of coming destruction.

Apollyon, whose name means destruction, is the fallen angelic beast who shall ascend from the bottomless pit as described in Revelation chapter 13. This beast has characteristics of the monoceros - a fierce <u>beast who is part lion</u> and also made up of other creatures.

Revelation 13:2 And the beast which I saw was like unto a leopard, and his feet were as the feet of a bear, and his mouth as the mouth of a lion…

Revelation 17:8 … and they that dwell on the earth shall wonder, whose names were not written in the book of life from the foundation of the world, when they behold the beast that was, and is not, and yet is.

Chapter 10 Blood, and Fire, and Vapour of Smoke

The day of the Lord is described in Acts 2:20. In verse 19 preceding the day of the Lord are prophesied signs portending that great and notable day of the Lord.

Acts 2:19 *AND I WILL SHEW WONDERS IN HEAVEN ABOVE, AND SIGNS IN THE EARTH BENEATH; <u>BLOOD, AND FIRE, AND VAPOUR OF SMOKE</u>:*

A wonder in heaven took place in January 2002 with the stellar pulse of supergiant star V838 Monocerotis. Just four months prior to this burst of light from Monocerotis another dramatic prophetic sign occurred on the earth. This sign took place on September 11, 2001. It was a sign on the earth of <u>blood, and fire, and vapour of smoke</u>. These two signs marked the beginning of this decade as the time that would soon see the return of Jesus Christ.

The event of September 11, 2001 was foretold by Isaiah who prophesied it to be the day of the great slaughter when the towers fall. It was described by the prophet Isaiah as a sign on the earth of the impending day of Lord.

Isaiah 30:25 *And there shall be upon every high mountain, and upon every high hill, rivers and streams of waters <u>in the day of the great slaughter, when the towers fall</u>. 26 Moreover the light of the moon shall be as the light of the sun, and the light of the sun shall be sevenfold, as the light of seven days, in the day that the LORD bindeth up the breach of his people, and healeth the stroke of their wound.*

In the next verse is the return of the Lord.

Isaiah 30:27 *Behold, <u>the name of the LORD cometh from far</u>, burning with his anger, and the burden thereof is heavy: his lips are full of indignation, and his tongue as a devouring fire:*

The name of the Lord is Jesus. Jesus shall come from far burning with his anger and his tongue shall be a devouring fire releasing punishment upon those left behind on the earth.

Isaiah 30:30 *And the LORD shall cause his glorious voice to be heard, and shall shew the lighting down of his arm, with the indignation of his anger, and with the flame of a devouring fire, with scattering, and tempest, and hailstones.*

The day of the great slaughter when the towers fall will be followed by a brief period revival in which the Lord brings healing to his people. Directly following this the wrath of God will be poured out on the earth.

The <u>day of the great slaughter when the towers fall</u> is a sign on the earth indicating that the DAY OF THE LORD is near.

Further details and prophetic references in scripture will be presented in later chapters as well as the appendix of this book regarding the day of the great slaughter when the towers fall.

Acts 2:19 prophesied that there would be two major signs indicating the imminent return of the Lord. One sign would be a wonder in the heavens, and the other would be a sign on the earth of blood, and fire, and vapour of smoke. The sign on earth of blood, and fire, and vapour of smoke also fulfills Isaiah's prophecy of "the day of great slaughter when towers fall." The stellar pulse of the supergiant star Monocerotis in January 2002 and the fall of the merchant city of the earth, the twin towers of the World Trade Center, in September 2001 were dramatic fulfillments of the prophecy of Acts 2:19. These two dramatic signs marked the first of this decade as the time near to the coming of Jesus Christ.

Chapter 11 Visit from the Cowboy Preacher

All work stations were empty as I entered my medical office the morning of September 11, 2001. Everyone was huddled around a small television set in a back office. On screen was a massive cloud of smoke billowing from one of towers of the World Trade Center. I stared wide-eyed as an airliner slammed into the second tower. The world was in shock.

I pondered the towers enveloped with fire and smoke. It was certain that all who were above the level where the planes hit had no hope of survival. It was inconceivable that both towers would soon be totally and utterly destroyed falling to the ground as if being suddenly unzipped in a crash that would shake the world. When tower one and then tower two fell, an unusual phrase prophetically whispered past my lips, *"Babylon is fallen, is fallen."*

Revelation chapter 18 defines the city Babylon as a <u>world trade center</u> that is violently destroyed by crashing to the ground in the end times. Babylon is described in scripture as a towering city of the world merchants and traders that violently crashes in ruin signaling the impending return of the Lord.

Revelation 18:21 *And a mighty angel took up a stone like a great millstone, and cast it into the sea, saying, Thus with violence shall that great city Babylon be thrown down, and shall be found no more at all.*

Revelation 18:15 *The **merchants** of these things, which were made rich by her, shall stand afar off for the fear of her torment, weeping and wailing, **16** And saying, Alas, alas, that great city, that was clothed in fine linen, and purple, and scarlet, and decked with gold, and precious stones, and pearls! **17** For in one hour so great riches is come to nought. And every shipmaster, and all the company in ships, and sailors, and as many as **<u>trade</u>** by sea, stood afar off, **18** And cried when they saw the smoke of her burning, saying, What city is like unto this great city! **19** And they cast dust on their heads, and cried, weeping and wailing,* *saying, Alas, alas, that great city, wherein were made rich all that had ships in the sea by reason of her costliness! for <u>in one hour is she made desolate</u>.*

A few weeks after September 11, 2001, I was visited by Glenn Smith the cowboy preacher. Glen flipped open his Bible to show me an amazing scripture where the prophet Isaiah foretold the fall of the World Trade Center as a sign of the pending return of the Lord.

Isaiah foretold the calamity and called this event <u>the day of the great slaughter when the towers fall</u>. It would be followed by a brief period of revival, and then the return of the Lord on the day of the Lord.

Isaiah 30:25 *And there shall be upon every high mountain, and upon every high hill, rivers and streams of waters in <u>the day of the great slaughter, when the towers fall</u>.* **26** *Moreover the light of the moon shall be as the light of the sun, and the light of the sun shall be sevenfold, as the light of seven days, in the day that the LORD bindeth up the breach of his people, and healeth the stroke of their wound.* **27** *Behold<u>, the name of the LORD cometh from far, burning with his anger</u>, and the burden thereof is heavy: his lips are full of indignation, and his tongue as a devouring fire:* **28** *And his breath, as an overflowing stream, shall reach to the midst of the neck, to sift the nations with the sieve of vanity: and <u>there shall be a bridle in the jaws of the people, causing them to err</u>.*

<u>Rivers and streams of waters</u> in verse 25 represent the anointing of the Spirit of the Lord being poured out in the last days. Verse 26 describes a brief period of revival. Verse 27 describes the coming of the Lord on the day of the Lord. Verse 28 describes the <u>strong delusion</u> that shall be on all those left behind on earth following the rapture of the Church, *"there shall be a bridle in the jaws of the people, causing them to err."*

The prophet Isaiah could see important future events with astonishing accuracy. Seven hundred years before the birth of Jesus

Christ, Isaiah precisely foretold the suffering our Lord Jesus would take to purchase our forgiveness and healing on the cross.

Isaiah 53:4 *Surely he hath borne our griefs, and carried our sorrows: yet we did esteem him stricken, smitten of God, and afflicted. **5** But he was wounded for our transgressions, he was bruised for our iniquities: the chastisement of our peace was upon him; and with his stripes we are healed. **6** All we like sheep have gone astray; we have turned every one to his own way; and the LORD hath laid on him the iniquity of us all.*

When the prophet Isaiah saw the suffering our Lord would endure he did not write in generalities. He clearly saw the coming event, even the whipping marks, the stripes placed on the back of Jesus that provided for our healing. The prophet Isaiah could also see thousands of years into the future to our current time and to see the key event that would signal the impending return of the King of Kings our Lord Jesus Christ.

The prophet Isaiah called that event precisely…

"…the day of the great slaughter when the towers fall." Isaiah 30:25

Isaiah foretold "the day of the great slaughter when the towers fall," as a signal that the return of Jesus Christ is at the door. It is no accident that a terrible day we know as 911 was the day Isaiah foretold as a signal that Revelation 911 is about to come upon the earth.

Chapter 12 The Mystery of 911

In the first book of the Bible, Genesis **9:11** tells of the first destruction on earth in the flood and God's promise to never again destroy the earth with a flood of water.

In the last book in the Bible Revelation **9:11** tells of the final destruction the release of the angelic beast Apollyon the Destroyer upon the inhabitants of the earth.

A day we know as **911** was the fulfillment of Isaiah's sign to portend the coming destruction of tribulation and the return of the Lord, *"...the day of the great slaughter when the towers fall." Isaiah 30:25*

But the middle book in the Bible Psalms **91:1** tells of our preservation on the day of the Lord as we are taken out of the destruction coming upon the earth.

Psalms 91:1 *He that dwelleth in the secret place of the most High shall abide under the shadow of the Almighty... 7 A thousand shall fall at thy side, and ten thousand at thy right hand; but it shall not come nigh thee. 8 Only with thine eyes shalt thou behold and see the reward of the wicked....10 There shall no evil befall thee...*

(Why shall no evil befall thee?) *11 For he shall give his angels charge over thee... 12 They shall bear thee up in their hands...*

Psalms 91 tells of the preservation of the elect on the day of the Lord. Ten thousand may fall beside you but the Lord shall send his angels to "bear you up." This is the rapture and escape of the Church on the day of the Lord.

Isaiah chapter 26 also tells of the events of the day of the Lord specifically resurrection, rapture, and the onset of tribulation punishment. These are preceded by the sign of a lofty city falling in destruction.

Note especially the following specific events that will be seen in the Isaiah passage.
- A lofty city falls in destruction signaling the imminent coming of the Lord, Verse 5
- Then after a brief period the events of the day of the Lord...

- Resurrection of the dead in Christ, Verse 19
- Rapture of the Church, Verse 20
- Punishment on those left behind… Tribulation, Verse 21

Isaiah 26:5 *For he bringeth down them that dwell on high; the <u>lofty city</u>, he layeth it low; he layeth it low, even to the ground; he bringeth it even to the dust.* ***19*** <u>*Thy dead men shall live*</u>*, together with my dead body shall they <u>arise</u>. Awake and sing, ye that dwell in dust: for thy dew is as the dew of herbs, and the earth shall cast out the dead.* ***20*** <u>*Come, my people, enter thou into thy chambers*</u>*, and shut thy doors about thee: hide thyself as it were for a little moment, until the indignation be overpast.* ***21*** *For, behold, the LORD cometh out of his place <u>to punish the inhabitants of the earth</u> for their iniquity…*

In verse 20, the Lord's people are taken into the chamber, which is the marriage supper of the Lamb and the rapture of the Church. This is the same chamber the five wise virgins enter in the parable of the ten virgins. For the foolish left behind there is not a second chance.

In verse 21 the purpose of tribulation is seen. The purpose is to punish the inhabitants left behind on the earth for their iniquity. Those left behind shall be an unrepentant people. They shall not repent during the punishment of tribulation no matter the severity of the plagues that come.

Revelation 9:20 *And the rest of the men which were not killed by these plagues <u>yet repented not</u> …****21*** <u>*Neither repented they*</u> *of their murders, nor of their sorceries, nor of their fornication, nor of their thefts.*

Revelation 16:10 *And the fifth angel poured out his vial upon the seat of the beast; and his kingdom was full of darkness; and they gnawed their tongues for pain…* ***11*** *And blasphemed the God of heaven because of their pains and their sores, and <u>repented not</u> of their deeds.*

Those left behind shall be an <u>unrepentant</u> people to the end. This is the reason of the admonition of Jesus, "*<u>Repent, for the kingdom of heaven is at hand</u>*" *Matthew 4:17*. The day of the Lord is coming and the Lord is not willing that any should perish but that all should come to repentance and the knowledge of our Lord Jesus Christ.

***2 Peter** 3:9 The Lord is not slack concerning his promise, as some men count slackness; but is longsuffering to us-ward, not willing that any should perish, but that <u>all should come to repentance</u>. **10** But the day of the Lord will come as a thief in the night…*

Chapter 13 The Vision of the Golden Ball

Acts chapter two tells of prophetic dreams and visions in the last days. The vision of the golden ball is one such vision that foretold the coming destruction of the World Trade Center. The destruction of the twin towers was a surprising shock to all the inhabitants of the earth. But the Lord had revealed the secret of this coming calamity to one of his servants years prior to the event through a vision, the vision of the golden ball.

Amos 3:7 Surely the Lord GOD will do nothing, but he revealeth his secret unto his servants the prophets.

In 2002, shortly after my evangelistic message was published in the newspaper explaining the prophetic significance of 911, I received a phone call from a former patient of several years. She began our conversation by telling me of her vision.

The prophetic nature of her vision and the phone call are real. This is not a novel.

"Dr. Gage I used to be your patient and after I read your article about the fall of the World Trade Center being a sign that the Lord shall soon return I had to call you.

You see I grew up in Manhattan. In my younger days I spent many wonderful afternoons enjoying Central Park, the museums, and the wonderful architecture. I loved Manhattan.

When the twin towers were constructed I saw them many times. But to me, they never seemed to fit in. The towers did not seem to be a real part of the city. They were so different and seemed not to be "Manhattan" but rather to be a city of their own.

One day, shortly after the twin towers were completed I was walking near them and looked up. Suddenly a huge golden ball appeared in a vision between the twin towers about a fourth of the way from the top.

I wondered in great amazement at this huge golden ball, wondering perhaps what it might mean. I looked so grand that I thought perhaps that it might break open and a great shower of confetti might be released from this amazing golden ball.

As I pondered for several minutes I said, "Lord, what is this golden ball?"

The Lord spoke, *"IT IS A WRECKING BALL."*

I carried this vision in my heart for a number of years and told no one. After I read your article about the prophetic significance of the fall of the World Trade Center, I knew that I had to call you and tell you about the vision."

On 911 demonized men had free reign to destroy the World Trade Center. This was not only a warning sign of coming tribulation, but a foretaste of tribulation itself when demonic forces will not only have free reign to bring destruction at ground zero but over the entire earth.

Chapter 14 THE DAY OF THE LORD

The day of the Lord is the linchpin attaching the wheel of our understanding to the mysterious timeline in the book of Revelation. Like the constant in an algebraic equation, the day of the Lord is a constant that enables us to group key events on the timeline of eschatological mystery. A complete understanding of the events that shall occur on the day of the Lord is essential to explaining accurately the sequence of end time events.

The book of Revelation contains a series of visions. Some key events are described repeatedly in more than one vision in different chapters in the book of Revelation.

Visions described in the book of Revelation are also frequently not described in chronological order. For example Revelation chapter 6 and 7 describe some of the events of the day of the Lord such as a great earthquake, the sun going dark, men hiding in caves and rocks, and the sealing of the 144,000 Jews who will be protected in the wilderness during the 3 & ½ year tribulation period. But in a later chapter, Revelation chapter 12, is the vision of an event that occurred much earlier in time. The chapter begins with a vision of the birth of Jesus Christ that occurred 2000 years ago. But later in that same chapter is seen an event previously described in chapter 7 of the book of Revelation as the nation of Israel is taken into the wilderness for protection during the 3&1/2 year tribulation. The book of Revelation was not laid out in chronological order. Key events may be described repeatedly in different visions and in different chapters in the book of Revelation.

Revelation chapter 9 describes yet another vision of the events that will occur on the day of the Lord as the bottomless pit is opened, the sun is darkened by smoke from the pit. Then the fallen angelic beast Apollyon arises from the pit to torture the inhabitants of the earth with an army of scorpion demons for the first 5 months of tribulation. Later in the book, Revelation chapter 18 describes a day preceding and portending the day of the Lord describing the crashing fall and destruction of the city which is the center of world trade, or as the prophet Isaiah described this same event... *"the day of the great slaughter when the towers fall."*

However, other portions of the book of Revelation do have specific chronological significance, for example the seven seals are opened in numerical sequence. The sounding of the seven trumpets follows chronologically the opening of the seven seals. Relating to this chronology, we shall see that the events of the day of the Lord begin with the opening of the sixth seal and continue through the sounding of the fifth trumpet. The events of this entire section of scripture from the sixth seal through the fifth trumpet all occur in the time period of one day, the day of the Lord.

The day of the Lord is a common thread running through the book of Revelation as well as other scriptures describing the end times. Events that occur on the day of the Lord are spokes in our wheel of understanding the mysterious timeline in the book of Revelation. Quick recognition of each of the events that will take place on the day of the Lord provides insight into the mysterious chronology and the many visions and events throughout the book of Revelation. This chapter will study the events that will take place on the day of the Lord.

The day of the Lord is coming. It is near.

Joel 2:1-2 *Blow ye the trumpet in Zion, and sound an alarm in my holy mountain: let all the inhabitants of the land tremble: for the day of the Lord cometh, for it is nigh at hand; A day of darkness and of gloominess, a day of clouds and of thick darkness,...*

Thousands of years ago Joel wrote this admonition from God to sound an alarm for the day of the Lord is coming. We are very much closer to that day now, and we should be sounding the alarm very much louder. That is why I am writing this book.

Zephaniah 1:14-18 *The <u>great day of the Lord is near</u>, it is near, and hasteth greatly, even the voice of the day of the Lord: the mighty man shall cry there bitterly. That day is a day of wrath, a day of trouble and* *distress, a day of wasteness and desolation, a day of darkness and gloominess, a day of clouds and thick darkness, A day of the trumpet and alarm against the fenced cities, and against the high towers. And I will bring distress upon men, that they shall walk like blind men, because they have sinned against the Lord: and their blood shall be poured out as dust, and their flesh as dung. Neither their silver nor their gold shall be able to deliver them in the day of the Lord's wrath: but the whole land shall be devoured by the fire of his jealousy: for he shall make even a <u>speedy riddance of all them that dwell in the land</u>.*

The DAY OF THE LORD is also called the day of the Lord's wrath. This will be an important detail when we look at the opening of the sixth seal in Revelation chapter 6. The day of the Lord will be the initial day of tribulation. The day of the Lord shall not be the initiation of a partial cleansing of wickedness from the earth, but rather a *"<u>speedy riddance of all</u> them that are left behind dwelling in the land."*

This speedy riddance shall be set in motion on the day of the Lord and will culminate at the end of the 3 & ½ year tribulation period with a battle that destroys all who have survived to this end point of tribulation. None shall survive this final battle that is described in both Revelation chapter 16 and also in chapter 19.

This battle is also known as Armegeddon. The battle is between the beast and his armies who are opposing Jesus Christ and the Lord's armies who accompany the King of Kings. The Lord and his armies are all riding on white horses as described in Revelation chapter 19. As a result of this battle the beast and the false prophet are cast into the lake of fire and the remnant of the beasts armies are slain by the sword coming out of the mouth of the Lord Jesus Christ. The fouls feed on their flesh. The armies of the beast who are slain in this battle are human.

Revelation 19:20 *And the beast was taken, and with him the false prophet that wrought miracles before him, with which he deceived them that had received the mark of the beast, and them that worshipped his image. These both were cast alive into a lake of fire burning with* *brimstone. **21** And the **<u>remnant</u>** <u>were slain</u> with the sword of him that sat upon the horse, which sword proceeded out of his mouth: and all the fowls were filled with their flesh.*

 The term remnant refers to *"a small surviving group"* according to one of the definitions given at Merriam Webster Dictionary online. At the end of tribulation "a small surviving group" shall be slain by the sword proceeding out of the mouth of the King of Kings.

 When this small surviving group is slain no one is left. All those left behind on earth after the rapture of the church shall all receive the mark of the beast. Then, just 3 & ½ years later, all with the mark of the beast shall all be dead. The Lord shall make a *"<u>speedy riddance</u>"* of all the wicked and the earth shall be totally cleansed.

 As it was in the days of Noah, so shall it be. All the wicked shall be destroyed and the earth shall be cleansed. Jesus Christ will then reign for 1000 years on an earth totally cleansed of all the wicked.

 The human armies of the beast who are slain in this battle at the end of tribulation all bear the mark of the beast. One thousand years later, at the conclusion of the 1000 year reign of Christ on the earth, these shall all be resurrected, judged, and cast into the lake of fire. After the 1000 year reign of Christ on earth ALL lost humans of all history will be resurrected at this same time to face the great white throne judgment. The result of the great white throne judgment is that these wicked shall all be cast into the lake of fire.

 This is further evidence that the beast and the false prophet are not human but rather fallen angels. The beast and the false prophet are thrown directly into the lake of fire at the conclusion of tribulation. If they were human they would, like their armies, be killed, resurrected after the 1000 year reign of Christ, and then face the great white throne judgment. The beast and the false prophet will not be at the white throne judgment because they are fallen angels, not lost humans. The white throne judgment is the final judgment for the entirety of all lost humans. All the wicked shall be cast into the lake of fire as seen in the following scripture.

Revelation 20:11 *And I saw a great white throne, and him that sat on it, from whose face the earth and the heaven fled away; and there was found no place for them.* ***12*** *And I saw the dead, small and great, stand before God; and the books were opened: and another book was opened, which is the book of life: and the dead were judged out of those things which were written in the books, according to their works.* ***13*** *And the sea gave up the dead which were in it; and death and hell delivered up the dead which were in them: and they were judged every man according to their works.* ***14*** *And death and hell were cast into the lake of fire. This is the <u>second death</u>.* ***15*** *And whosoever was not found written in the book of life was cast into the lake of fire.*

Note that this second resurrection is also referred to as <u>the second death</u>.

A review of the end time resurrections helps place them into proper perspective in regards to the day of the Lord. The <u>first</u> resurrection is of the righteous, those in Christ. This resurrection takes place on the day of the Lord. This resurrection is directly followed by the rapture of the church on the initial day of tribulation, the day of the Lord. The next resurrection is the special case of the two witnesses who are killed by the beast Apollyon 1260 days after the onset of tribulation. The resurrection of the two witnesses takes place after their bodies have been on display for 3 & ½ days during which the inhabitants of the earth rejoice because these two witnesses prophesied the punishments of tribulation upon the people. When they are raised and ascend into heaven, great fear comes upon the people.

The final resurrection is also called the "second death" and does not take place until after the tribulation and after the 1000 year reign of Christ on earth. This is the resurrection of the wicked, those who have denied Christ, throughout all history. This resurrection takes place at the time of the great white throne judgment. Those who are resurrected at this time will all be judged and cast into the lake of fire.

Regarding the resurrection of the righteous, those in Christ, 1 Thessalonians chapters 4 & 5 explain that the dead in Christ shall rise first and then the rapture of the church shall occur. These events are defined in this scripture passage as events of *"the day of the Lord,"* which shall come *"like a thief in the night."* Note that this resurrection of the righteous is the <u>first</u> resurrection. The prophet Isaiah writes of this resurrection and that he himself shall be raised at this time as we shall see when we study Isaiah 26:19.

As a note to those who study eschatology fervently, the scripture passage in Revelation 20:4-6 would at first appear to be another different and later resurrection occurring after tribulation. However, it actually refers again to the resurrection of the dead in Christ on the initial day of tribulation, the day of the Lord. Note in this passage that those resurrected would include all the dead in Christ throughout history and even including the prophet Isaiah. Some of these were beheaded for their faith, and none worshiped the beast, and none took his mark for they "escaped all these things" to stand before the son of Man at the throne in heaven. Verse 6 clearly defines the resurrection of Revelation 20:4-6 as the <u>FIRST</u> resurrection. This is the resurrection that preceeds the rapture of the church. If this were a second or later resurrection it would not be called the <u>first</u> resurrection.

Revelation 20:6 *Blessed and holy is he that hath part in the <u>first</u> resurrection: on such the second death hath no power, but they shall be priests of God and of Christ, and shall reign with him a thousand years.*

There is however a second later resurrection which is termed the second death. This is the resurrection of all the wicked at the time of the great white throne judgment.

The initial day of tribulation will be the day of the Lord. The sun shall be darkened, a great earthquake will shake the entire earth, those left behind after the rapture shall hide in caves and rock in great fear.

Isaiah 2:12 *For the day of the LORD of hosts shall be upon every one that is proud and lofty, and upon every one that is lifted up; and he shall be brought low:* **13** *And upon all the cedars of Lebanon, that are high and lifted up, and upon all the oaks of Bashan,* **14** *And upon all the high mountains, and upon all the hills that are lifted up,* **15** *And upon every high tower, and upon every fenced wall,* **16** *And upon all the ships of Tarshish, and upon all pleasant pictures.* **17** *And the loftiness of man shall be bowed down, and the haughtiness of men shall be made low: and the LORD alone shall be exalted in that day.* **18** *And the idols he shall utterly abolish.* **19** *And they shall go into the holes of the rocks, and into the caves of the earth, for fear of the LORD, and for the glory of his majesty, when he ariseth to shake terribly the earth.* **20** *In that day a man shall cast his idols of silver, and his idols of gold, which they made each one for himself to worship, to the moles and to the bats;* **21** *To go into the clefts of the rocks, and into the tops of the ragged rocks, for fear of the LORD, and for the glory of his majesty, when he ariseth to shake terribly the earth.*

The opening of the sixth seal in the following scripture also describes events of the day of the LORD.

Revelation 6:12 *And I beheld when he had opened the sixth seal, and, lo, there was a great earthquake; and the sun became black as sackcloth of hair, and the moon became as blood;*

Revelation 6:15 *And the kings of the earth, and the great men, and the rich men, and the chief captains, and the mighty men, and every bondman, and every free man, hid themselves in the dens and in the rocks of the mountains;* **16** *And said to the mountains and rocks, Fall on us, and hide us from the face of him that sitteth on the throne, and from the wrath of the Lamb:* **17** *For the great day of his wrath is come; and who shall be able to stand?*

The great and notable day of the Lord is also known as the great day of his wrath. Acts chapter 2 describes other events that will mark the day of the Lord.

Acts 2:20 *THE SUN SHALL BE TURNED INTO DARKNESS AND THE MOON INTO BLOOD, BEFORE* (or in the face of) *THAT GREAT AND NOTABLE DAY OF THE LORD.*

Acts 2:21 AND IT SHALL COME TO PASS, THAT WHOSOEVER SHALL CALL ON THE NAME OF THE LORD SHALL BE SAVED.

On the day of the LORD there will be a supernatural proclamation of the GOSPEL OF GRACE released from the Kingdom of Heaven. The final call of grace shall be preached by a great angel as prophesied in Revelation 14:6. All who call on the name of the Lord as this angelic preaching goes forth shall be saved. The harvest of souls on that day will be greater than any day in history. It shall be a sovereign harvest of God accomplished by a great angel in fulfillment of the prophecy of Jesus…

Matthew 24:14 *And this gospel of the kingdom shall be preached in all the world for a witness unto all nations; and then shall the end come.*

The fulfillment of the prophecy of Matthew 24:14 is seen in John's vision of angelic preaching in the following scripture, Revelation 14:6. The preaching of a great angel shall reach every ear on earth within the space of one hour on the day of the Lord. The day of the Lord is the day that "the hour of his judgment is come." The rapture of the church shall immediately follow this angelic preaching as the dispensation of grace comes to an end.

Revelation 14:6 *And I saw another angel fly in the midst of heaven, having the everlasting <u>gospel</u> to preach unto them that dwell on the earth, and to every nation, and kindred, and tongue, and people, 7 Saying with a loud voice, Fear God, and give glory to him; <u>for the hour of his judgment is come</u>: and worship him that made heaven, and earth, and the sea, and the fountains of waters.*

Can you picture the events of the day of the LORD? The sun goes dark, the moon turns blood red, an earthquake shakes every mountain and island on earth and in the midst of this an angel is flying all over the earth yelling in a loud voice, "FEAR GOD!..."

Many will fear God, and like the thief on the cross, call on the name of Jesus at the final moment. The preaching of the angel of Revelation 14:6, will be the most dramatic gospel message ever preached and will fulfill completely Matthew 24:14 on that great and notable day of the LORD. It is the grace of God, a sovereign move of God, that will literally shake the earth and release from the kingdom of heaven this revival of grace giving every inhabitant on earth a final opportunity of salvation. When this final call of grace is finished the dispensation of grace shall be at an end.

The manifestations of earthquake, total darkness, and resurrection of the dead in Christ occurs on the great and notable day of the Lord. The resurrection of the dead on that day will immediately precede the rapture of the church as described in the following passage from 1 Thessalonians chapter 4. These events will occur on the day of the LORD as noted as the passage continues with the next few verses in chapter 5.

1Thessalonians 4:15 For this we say unto you by the word of the Lord, that we which are alive and remain unto the coming of the Lord shall not prevent them which are asleep. 16 For the Lord himself shall descend from heaven with a shout, with the voice of the archangel, and with the trump of God: and the dead in Christ shall rise first: 17 <u>Then we which are alive and remain shall be caught up together with them in the clouds</u>, to meet the Lord in the air: and so shall we ever be with the Lord. 18 Wherefore comfort one another with these words:

Chapter 5:1 *But of the times and the seasons, brethren, ye have no need that I write unto you. 2 For yourselves know perfectly that* **<u>the day of the Lord</u>** *so cometh as a thief in the night.*

NOTE CAREFULLY THIS IMPORTANT KEY DETAIL. The above passage clearly identifies this fact… THE <u>RAPTURE</u> OF THE CHURCH OCCURS ON <u>THE DAY OF THE LORD</u>.

The resurrection of the dead in Christ, followed by the rapture of the church, and the onset of tribulation punishment are all events of the day of the Lord. These events are also seen in the following vision by Isaiah.

Isaiah 26:19-21 *Thy dead men shall <u>live together with my dead body, shall they arise</u>. Awake and sing, ye that dwell in dust: for thy dew is as the dew of herbs, and the earth shall cast out the dead. <u>Come my people, enter thou into thy chambers</u>, and shut thy doors about thee; hide thyself as it were for a little moment, until the indignation be overpast. For, behold, the <u>Lord cometh out of his place to punish the inhabitants of the earth</u> for their iniquity…*

These events take place on the day of the Lord.
- Resurrection of the dead in Christ.
- Rapture of the church which is taken into the marriage chamber.
- The onset of tribulation punishment upon the inhabitants of the earth who have been left behind outside the marriage chamber.

After the rapture of the church, another event occurs on the day of the Lord. The bottomless pit is opened and the beast Apollyon ascends to torment those left behind and forces all those left behind to take his mark, the mark of the beast. The bottomless pit is opened on the day of the Lord and the sun is darkened by smoke from the pit as seen in the following scripture passage.

Revelation 9:1 *And the fifth angel sounded, and I saw a star fall from heaven unto the earth: and to him was given the key of the bottomless pit.* ***2*** *And he opened the bottomless pit; and there arose a smoke out of the pit, as the smoke of a great furnace; <u>and the sun and the air were darkened</u> by reason of the smoke of the pit.*

How do we know that the opening of the bottomless pit shall occur on the day of the Lord? First of all, we know that the sun goes dark on the day of the Lord and as noted above in Revelation 9:2 that the sun is darkened by smoke from the pit.

We also know from Revelation chapter 13:5 that the beast shall reign on earth for 42 months. This is a clue. 42 months is the entire length of the tribulation period, three and one half years. Since the tribulation lasts exactly this long, three and one half years, we know that the beast must be released from the bottomless pit on the first day of tribulation in order to reign on earth for the full 42 months. The day tribulation begins is the day of the Lord. We therefore know that the bottomless pit must be opened to release the beast Apollyon on the day of the Lord. The beast shall then reign on earth for the entirety of the tribulation period of 42 months, or 3 and ½ years.

In Revelation 9:11 the beast Apollyon ascends out of the bottomless pit. This event occurs as the pit is opened on the day of the Lord with the sounding of the fifth trumpet. The events of the day of the Lord are first seen with the opening of the sixth seal and culminate with the sounding of the fifth trumpet as Apollyon releases his hoard of scorpion demons to torment mankind for the first 5 months of the tribulation period. These events all occur or begin on a day the Bible defines as the day of the Lord.

The vision of another and different important event that shall take place on the day of the Lord is seen in Zechariah chapters 12 & 14. One the day of the Lord the feet of Jesus shall stand on the Mount of Olives. Jerusalem shall be under attack. 144,000 Jews shall flee to the Mount of Olives and shall look upon Jesus whom they have pierced and weep as they receive him as their Lord. The Mount of Olives shall split forming a valley of escape into the wilderness for the 144,000 who shall flee through the valley in the mountain.

This event in which Jesus stands on the Mount of Olives is commonly considered to occur at the end of tribulation in most traditional teachings but clearly occurs instead at the onset of tribulation. The 144,000 would have no need to flee into the wilderness for 3 & ½ years of protection if tribulation were at an end. They shall flee through the valley of the mountain into the wilderness away from Jerusalem at the onset of tribulation. These events do indeed occur on the day of the Lord at the onset of the tribulation period and on the same day as the rapture of the church.

Zechariah 14:1 *Behold,* **<u>the day of the LORD</u>** *cometh, and thy spoil shall be divided in the midst of thee.* *2 For I will gather all nations against Jerusalem to battle; and the city shall be taken,… 3 Then shall the LORD go forth, and fight against those nations, as when he fought in the day of battle.* *4* **<u>And his feet shall stand in that day upon the mount of Olives</u>***, and the mount of Olives shall cleave in the midst thereof toward the east and toward the west, and there shall be a very great valley; and half of the mountain shall remove toward the north, and half of it toward the south.* *5 And* <u>*ye shall flee to the valley*</u> *of the mountains…*

Zechariah 12:10 *… and they shall look upon me whom they have pierced, and they shall mourn for him, as one mourneth for his only son, and shall be in bitterness for him, as one that is in bitterness for his firstborn.*

Events of the day of the Lord.
- Jerusalem is under attack.
- Jesus stands on the Mount of Olives.
- 144,000 Jews flee Jerusalem and meet Jesus on the Mount of Olives.
- The 144,000 look upon Jesus and weep as they receive him as Lord.
- The Mount of Olives splits forming a valley as a way of escape.
- The 144,000 are sealed in their forehead with the seal of God's protection and they flee though the valley of the mountain into the wilderness to special place prepared for them where they shall be nourished for 3 & ½ years.

THESE EVENTS OCCUR AT THE ONSET OF TRIBULATION, NOT AT THE END OF TRIBULATION.

Chapter 15 The Kingdom of Heaven Revival
A Final Proclamation of Grace

When the final proclamation of the gospel of grace has been completed, the dispensation of grace shall be at an end. Jesus proclaims this great mystery in Matthew 24:14.

Matthew 24:14 And this gospel of the kingdom shall be preached in all the world for a witness unto all nations; and then shall the end come.

Many teach that because some nations and peoples have not yet been reached with the gospel message that the Lord could not return today. When we fully understand the mystery of Matthew 24:14 we know that the Lord could indeed return today. Nothing is impossible with God, even the supernatural preaching of the gospel to reach all peoples of the earth could occur in one hour. Nothing is impossible with God.

Who shall preach the final gospel message so that the gospel shall have reached every nation, and kindred, and tongue, and people? This is a clue to the mystery. Many events and mysteries in the book of Revelation involve the activity of angels. Many mysteries are unsolved because people do not realize that it shall be an angel and not a human who shall fulfill the prophecy.

The most dramatic worldwide revival ever to be preached will not come forth from the ministry of any man. This great revival will be a sovereign act of the grace of God. The final great revival will come directly out of the Kingdom of Heaven.

A great angel shall be sent cross the earth as the hour God's judgment has come to preach the final gospel message. After this final gospel message goes forth across the earth, the dispensation of grace shall come to a close, the rapture of the Church shall take place, and the punishment of tribulation shall be released upon the earth.

Revelation 14:6-7 *And I saw another angel fly in the midst of heaven, having the <u>everlasting gospel</u> to preach unto them that dwell on the earth, and to every nation, and kindred, and tongue, and people, Saying with a loud voice, Fear God, and give glory to him; for <u>the hour of his judgment is come</u>: and worship him that made heaven, and earth, and the sea, and the fountains of waters.*

On the DAY OF THE LORD as the sun goes black, as the moon turns blood red, as a great earthquake shakes every island and mountain on earth, a great revival will be preached from the Kingdom of Heaven. This revival of the grace of God, will be preached by an angel to all nations in every language as the hour of God's judgment comes upon the earth.

This angel of mercy will preach the everlasting gospel to all nations in all languages. The angel will preach from the midst of heaven in a loud voice so all the inhabitants of the earth may hear. Even deaf ears will pop open to hear this angelic preaching. All inhabitants on earth will have a final chance to hear the gospel and receive Jesus Christ as the dispensation of grace comes to an end.

And it shall come to pass on the DAY OF THE LORD that whosoever shall call on the name of the Lord Jesus at that final hour will be saved. The Kingdom of Heaven Revival, the final Proclamation of the Gospel Grace preached by an angel will be the fulfillment of the prophecy of Jesus…

Matthew 24:14 *And this gospel of the kingdom shall be preached in all the world for a witness unto all nations; and then shall the end come.*

Revelation 14:6 *And I saw another angel fly in the midst of heaven, having the everlasting gospel to preach unto them that dwell on the earth, and to every nation, and kindred, and tongue, and people, 7 Saying with a loud voice, Fear God, and give glory to him; for the hour of his judgment is come: and worship him that made heaven, and earth, and the sea, and the fountains of waters.*

On the day of the Lord as the sun goes dark and the earth shakes a powerful angel will fly across the earth at the last hour preaching the everlasting gospel to every ear on earth. The angel will shout "FEAR GOD…"

Many will fear God on the great and notable day of the Lord. Many shall call on the name of Jesus for salvation as the final proclamation of the gospel of grace takes place and the dispensation of grace comes to a close. The everlasting gospel preached across the earth as the sun goes dark and the earth shakes shall bring in the greatest harvest of souls ever witnessed. It shall be the final harvest, and it shall come to pass that WHOSOEVER SHALL CALL ON THE NAME OF THE LORD SHALL BE SAVED.

Acts 2:20-21 THE SUN SHALL BE TURNED INTO DARKNESS AND THE MOON INTO BLOOD, BEFORE THAT GREAT AND NOTABLE DAY OF THE LORD. AND IT SHALL COME TO PASS, THAT WHOSOEVER SHALL CALL ON THE NAME OF THE LORD SHALL BE SAVED.

Chapter 16 Sequence of End Time Events
Opening the Seven Seals

The sequence of end time events is seen in the opening of the seven seals. The seven seals are opened in chronological order. This is key to understanding the chronology or sequence of end time events including the rapture of the church. The rapture of the church occurs before the wrath of God begins to pour out upon those left behind dwelling upon the earth. The event of the wrath of God being poured out is also termed, "the avenging of the blood of the martyrs."

Only the Lord Jesus is worthy to open the seals…

Revelation 5:1 And I saw in the right hand of him that sat on the throne a book written within and on the backside, sealed with seven seals. 2 And I saw a strong angel proclaiming with a loud voice, Who is worthy to open the book, and to loose the seals thereof? 3 And no man in heaven, nor in earth, neither under the earth, was able to open the book, neither to look thereon. 4 And I wept much, because no man was found worthy to open and to read the book, neither to look thereon. 5 And one of the elders saith unto me, Weep not: behold, the Lion of the tribe of Juda, the Root of David, hath prevailed to open the book, and to loose the seven seals thereof.

The Lion of Juda, the Root of David, has prevailed to open the book, and to loose the seven seals on the scroll. Only Jesus Christ is worthy to loose the seals and open the scroll.

What does the scroll contain? The answer to this mystery is key to understanding.

The scroll contains the pronouncements of tribulation punishment, also known as the avenging of the blood of the martyrs, that shall be poured out upon those who dwell on the earth. This is why only the spotless Lamb of God, the sinless Lord Jesus Christ is worthy to loose the seven seals and open the scroll. Only the sinless one can pronounce this punishment upon the earth.

Consider Jesus addressing this concept that only a sinless one can pronounce punishment as seen in the following scripture passage.

***John 8:3** And the scribes and Pharisees brought unto him a woman taken in adultery; and when they had set her in the midst, **4** They say unto him, Master, this woman was taken in adultery, in the very act. **5** Now Moses in the law commanded us, that such should be stoned: but what sayest thou? **6** This they said, tempting him, that they might have to accuse him. But Jesus stooped down, and with his finger wrote on the ground, as though he heard them not. **7** So when they continued asking him, he lifted up himself, and said unto them, He that is without sin among you, let him first cast a stone at her.*

In the above passage the only one present without sin was Jesus Christ. Only Jesus was worthy to pronounce and release punishment upon the woman caught in adultery. Jesus could condemn her, but he would not. During the dispensation of grace Jesus would not release punishment upon the woman caught in adultery. She had the opportunity to receive forgiveness and freedom from condemnation through Jesus Christ. Jesus could release punishment upon her but he would not. It was in the dispensation of grace.

A time is coming when the dispensation of grace will be over at the onset of the tribulation period. This will be the appointed time when the punishment of tribulation, the avenging of the blood of the martyrs, will be poured out upon those dwelling upon the earth.

Jesus Christ, the only one without sin, is the only one worthy to loose the seals and open the scroll releasing tribulation punishment upon the earth. Jesus is the only one worthy of releasing this terrible punishment and he will do so because the dispensation of grace will be at an end. If the dispensation of grace was not indeed finished at that point, Jesus would not release the punishment on the earth just as he did not release punishment upon the woman caught in adultery during the dispensation of grace.

After the elect are transported to heaven on the first day of tribulation the dispensation of grace will be over. Tribulation punishment, the avenging of the blood of the martyrs, will be poured out upon those left behind dwelling on the earth. Jesus is the only one worthy of releasing the avenging of the blood of the martyrs, the wrath of God, upon those left behind.

It is also key to understand that the blood of the martyrs to be avenged includes the blood of Jesus Christ shed on the cross. It also includes the blood of all the other martyrs slain for the cause of Christ from the cross until the onset of tribulation when the blood of each and every martyr shall be avenged.

The following question reveals a very important mystery and key to understanding… When is a scroll with seven seals unfurled?

The answer is elementary and also vital to a true understanding of the sequence of end time events in the book of Revelation. A scroll with seven seals is not unfurled until the seventh or final seal is loosed, then and only then can the pronouncements of tribulation punishment written on the scroll be poured out upon the wicked left behind dwelling upon the earth.

The opening of the seals is in preparation for punishment. That punishment will be the avenging of the blood of the martyrs.

The opening of each seal makes preparation for the punishment that shall be poured out when the scroll is finally opened. When the seventh or final seal is loosed then and only then shall the scroll be unfurled, releasing the punishment of tribulation upon those dwelling upon the earth. Then and only then shall the avenging of the blood of the martyrs commence. As the seals are opened we see recurrent clues that the punishment shall not yet be poured forth until the final or seventh seal is opened at the appointed time.

The opening of the first four seals. With each of first four seals the four horsemen, who are fallen angels, are each granted commissions to go forth and hurt the earth. But these four angels given to hurt the earth will later be told to wait and not begin their ride of destruction until certain events which shall take place at the opening of the sixth seal as we shall see. These events will provide for the escape of God's elect and the rapture of the church.

***Revelation 6:1** And I saw when the Lamb opened one of the seals, and I heard, as it were the noise of thunder, one of the four beasts saying, Come and see. **2** And I saw, and behold a white horse: and he that sat on him had a bow; and a crown was given unto him: and he went forth conquering, and to conquer.*

***Revelation 6:3** And when he had opened the second seal, I heard the second beast say, Come and see. **4** And there went out another horse that was red: and power was given to him that sat thereon to take peace from the earth, and that they should kill one another: and there was given unto him a great sword.*

***Revelation 6:5** And when he had opened the third seal, I heard the third beast say, Come and see. And I beheld, and lo a black horse; and he that sat on him had a pair of balances in his hand. **6** And I heard a voice in the midst of the four beasts say, A measure of wheat for a penny, and three measures of barley for a penny; and see thou hurt not the oil and the wine.*

***Revelation 6:7** And when he had opened the fourth seal, I heard the voice of the fourth beast say, Come and see. **8** And I looked, and behold a pale horse: and his name that sat on him was Death, and Hell followed with him. And power was given unto them over the fourth part of the earth, to kill with sword, and with hunger, and with death, and with the beasts of the earth.*

Who are these four horsemen? The clue is found in verse 8 above. One of the horsemen is named Death. Death is a fallen angel and the other horsemen are fallen angels also. How do we know this?

To explain this mystery we must consider the question. What is the destiny of the one named Death? The destiny of Death reveals a solution to the mystery as the one named Death shares a destiny of others who are also <u>fallen angels</u>.

Satan is a fallen angel. Satan's ultimate destiny shall be the lake of fire. (Revelation 20:10) The beast Apollyon and the false prophet are both fallen angels whose destiny is the lake of fire. (Revelation 19:20) Death is the last enemy to be destroyed and is also cast into the lake of fire. (Revelation 20:14) Death, Satan, Apollyon, and the false prophet are all enemies. Death is the <u>last enemy</u> to be destroyed which is also referred to in 1Cor.15:2. Like Satan, Apollyon, and the false prophet, Death is also a fallen angel with a common destiny, the lake of fire.

The four horsemen are <u>fallen</u> angels. Each of these <u>four angels</u> is given a commission to <u>hurt the earth</u>. Later we shall see that these four angels must wait to begin their ride of destruction until after preparatory events described in the opening of sixth and seventh seals. The fact that the punishment of tribulation is not yet to begin is also further described in the opening of the fifth seal.

Revelation 6:9 *And when he had opened the fifth seal, I saw under the altar the souls of them that were slain for the word of God, and for the testimony which they held:* ***10*** *And they cried with a loud voice, saying, How long, O Lord, holy and true, dost thou not judge and avenge our blood on them that dwell on the earth?* ***11*** *And white robes were given unto every one of them; and it was said unto them, that they should* <u>*rest yet for a little season*</u>*,...*

The opening of the fifth seal releases <u>prayers of the saints</u> who were slain. The prayers of the saints call on the Lord to judge and <u>avenge their blood</u> on them that dwell on the earth. The response of God to these prayers of the saints calling for the avenging of their blood is that they must <u>wait</u> a little longer. The avenging of their blood cannot yet begin. Next, we shall review again the opening of the fifth seal…

Revelation 6:9 *And when he had opened the fifth seal, I saw under the altar the souls of them that were slain for the word of God, and for* *the testimony which they held: **10** And they cried with a loud voice, saying, How long, O Lord, holy and true, dost thou not judge and avenge our blood on them that dwell on the earth? **11** And white robes were given unto every one of them; and it was said unto them, that they <u>should rest yet for a little season,</u> <u>until their fellowservants also and their brethren, that should be killed as they were, should be fulfilled</u>.*

The onset of tribulation, which is the "avenging of the blood of the martyrs," shall not begin <u>until the last martyr has been slain.</u> When the last martyr ever to be slain has been killed then tribulation will begin. The exception shall be the specific case of the two witnesses who are not slain by humans but rather by the fallen angelic beast Apollyon.

The avenging of the blood of the martyrs shall not take place until all martyrs throughout history past, present, <u>and future</u> have been slain. Then and only then shall the blood of all the martyrs be avenged all at once. The few scriptures that would appear to indicate that martyrs shall be killed during tribulation are explained by the death of <u>just the two witnesses</u>.

The point of the fifth seal is this:
- Tribulation has not yet begun.
- The prayers of the martyred saints are crying out for the punishment of tribulation to begin to avenge their blood.
- The Lord says that tribulation will not start until <u>all</u> martyrs have been slain.
- The fifth seal is proof that no martyrs will be slain after the initiation of tribulation.

Later in this chapter, on page 105, we shall see that tribulation, the avenging of the blood, shall begin when the first trumpet sounds exactly ½ hour after the opening of the seventh seal. At that point there shall be 3 & ½ years of tribulation which is the entirety of the tribulation period. The day of these events is the day of the Lord, which also encompasses events though the sounding of the fifth trumpet when the bottomless pit is opened and the beast ascends. If this timeline does not seem clear, please review the clue to this mystery on page 89 which covers the fact that the beast who ascends from the bottomless pit will reign on earth a full 42 months which is the entire length of the tribulation period.

Next, after the fifth seal is opened, then the sixth seal is opened and the events of the DAY OF THE LORD occur on the earth in the final preparation for the punishment of tribulation to be poured out. The following is a summary of some of the many events that shall occur on the day of the Lord at the opening of the sixth seal.

Events of the day of the Lord:
- The sun goes dark.
- A great earthquake shakes every mountain and island.
- An angel preaches the gospel across the earth in one hour giving all the inhabitants of the earth a final call of grace, a final chance at salvation.
- It shall come to pass that whosoever shall call on the name of the Lord shall be saved.
- Every eye sees Jesus coming on the clouds in power and glory and Jesus sends his angels to gather the elect and transport them off the earth to stand before him at the throne room in an event commonly called the rapture of the Church.
- The bottomless pit is opened and the beast Apollyon ascends to dominate and torture those left behind. He forces <u>all</u> to take the mark of the beast.
- 144,000 of the children of Israel receive a seal of the Lords protection and are taken into the wilderness to a place of protection to be nourished and protected there for the full 3 and ½ years of tribulation punishment.
- Those not taken off the earth in the rapture are left behind. They hide in caves and rocks seeking to hide themselves from the face of the Lord. They do not wonder why everyone has disappeared or vanished in the rapture, they cower in caves and rocks crying, "Hide us from the face of Him who sits on the throne." For…

Revelation 1:7 *…every eye shall see him, and they also which pierced him: and all kindreds of the earth shall wail because of him. Even so, Amen.*

Revelation 6:12 *And I beheld when he had opened the sixth seal, and, lo, there was a great earthquake; and the sun became black as sackcloth of hair, and the moon became as blood;*

Revelation 6:14 *And the heaven departed as a scroll when it is rolled together; and every mountain and island were moved out of their places.* ***15*** *And the kings of the earth, and the great men, and the rich men, and the chief captains, and the mighty men, and every bondman, and every free man,* <u>*hid themselves in the dens and in the rocks*</u> *of the mountains;* ***16*** *And said to the mountains and rocks, Fall on us, and* <u>*hide us from the face of him that sitteth on the throne*</u>*, and from the wrath of the Lamb:* ***17*** *For the great day of his wrath is come; and who shall be able to stand?*

The DAY OF THE LORD is also called the <u>great day of his wrath</u>. It is also described in this passage from Isaiah.

Isaiah 2:12 *For* <u>*the day of the LORD*</u> *of hosts shall be upon every one that is proud and lofty, and upon every one that is lifted up; and he shall be brought low…* ***17*** *And the loftiness of man shall be bowed down, and the haughtiness of men shall be made low: and the LORD alone shall be exalted in that day.* ***18*** *And the idols he shall utterly abolish.* ***19*** *And they shall go into the holes of the rocks, and into the caves of the earth, for fear of the LORD, and for the glory of his majesty, when he ariseth* <u>*to shake terribly the earth*</u>*.* ***20*** *In that day a man shall cast his idols of silver, and his idols of gold, which they made each one for himself to worship, to the moles and to the bats;* ***21*** *To* <u>*go into the clefts of the rocks, and into the tops of the ragged rocks, for fear of the LORD*</u>*, and for the glory of his majesty, when he ariseth to shake terribly the earth.*

After the sixth seal is opened additional events on the day of the Lord are described in Revelation chapter 7 which provide for the evacuation and protection of God's people. The people of God who are protected include the 144,000 Jews taken into the wilderness and also the church that is raptured. These evacuations of God's people occur as described in Revelation chapter 7 prior to the opening of the seventh seal in Revelation chapter 8.

Revelation 7:2 *And I saw another angel ascending from the east, having the seal of the living God: and he cried with a loud voice to the* <u>four angels, to whom it was given to hurt the earth</u> *and the sea,* **3** *Saying,* <u>Hurt not the earth</u>, *neither the sea, nor the trees,* <u>till we have sealed the servants of our God in their foreheads</u>. **4** *And I heard the number of them which were sealed: and there were sealed an hundred and forty and four thousand of all the tribes of the children of Israel.*

Note again in the above passage that the <u>four angels</u> who have been given a commission to hurt the earth are still not yet allowed to begin hurting the earth. Why? The 144,000 must first be given a seal of God's protection in their forehead. Also there must first occur the next event described in chapter 7. This great event is the rapture of the Church which is described as a great multitude are taken out of tribulation that is beginning upon the earth and these shall stand before the Lord at the throne.

Revelation 7:9 *After this I beheld, and, lo,* <u>a great multitude</u>, *which no man could number, of all nations, and kindreds, and people, and tongues,* <u>stood</u> *before the throne, and* <u>before the Lamb</u>, *clothed with white robes, and palms in their hands;* **10** *And cried with a loud voice, saying, Salvation to our God which sitteth upon the throne, and unto the Lamb.* **11** *And all the angels stood round about the throne, and about the elders and the four beasts, and fell before the throne on their faces, and worshipped God,* **12** *Saying, Amen: Blessing, and glory, and wisdom, and thanksgiving, and honour, and power, and might, be unto our God for ever and ever. Amen.* **13** *And one of the elders answered, saying unto me, What are these which are arrayed in white robes? and whence came they?* **14** *And I said unto him, Sir, thou knowest. And he said to me, These are they which* <u>came out of great tribulation</u>, *and have washed their robes, and made them white in the blood of the Lamb.*

At this point God's people are now protected. The Church has been raptured to heaven, and the 144,000 have the seal of God placed on their foreheads and are taken to a place in the wilderness for protection on earth. Then and only then is the seventh seal opened. As the seventh seal is opened there is a great calm before the storm, a silence in heaven that lasts half an hour before the avenging of the blood upon those dwelling upon the earth commences.

The Calm Before the Storm... *Revelation 8:1 And when he had opened the seventh seal, there was silence in heaven about the space of half an hour.*

Revelation 8:1 And when he had opened the seventh seal, there was silence in heaven about the space of half an hour. 2 And I saw the seven angels which stood before God; and to them were given seven trumpets. 3 And another <u>angel came and stood at the altar, having a golden censer</u>; and there was given unto him much incense, that he should offer it <u>with the prayers of all saints</u> upon the golden altar which was before the throne. 4 And the smoke of the incense, which came with the prayers of the saints, ascended up before God out of the angel's hand. 5 And <u>the angel took the censer, and filled it with fire of the altar, and cast it into the earth</u>: and there were voices, and thunderings, and lightnings, and an earthquake. 6 And the seven angels which had the seven trumpets prepared themselves to sound.

Note in the above scripture that an angel stands at the alter with a golden censer. A censer is a large metal ball suspended from a chain in which incense is burned. The ball is usually swung back and forth by someone holding the chain as the smoke of incense is released from the censer. This is frequently seen in processions and ceremonies in the Catholic Church.

In the scripture above the angel takes fire from the altar and places it in the censer. The <u>prayers of the saints</u> are also offered with this incense. The mystery involved is the question, What are these prayers of the saints requesting? The answer refers back to the opening of the fifth seal. At the opening of the fifth seal the prayers of the saints were calling for the <u>avenging of the blood</u> of the martyrs. These prayers are offered with the incense. The censer is then cast into the earth and the <u>avenging of the blood of the martyrs</u> is thus released upon the earth.

Revelation 8:7 *The first angel sounded, and there followed hail and fire <u>mingled with blood</u>, and they were cast upon the earth: and the third part of trees was burnt up, and all green grass was burnt up. 8And the second angel sounded, and as it were a great mountain burning with fire was cast into the sea: and <u>the third part of the sea became blood</u>;*

In the above scripture, hail and fire are mingled with <u>blood</u> and the sea becomes <u>blood</u> because the <u>avenging of the blood</u> of the martyrs has begun. As described in the opening of the fifth seal, we know that all martyrs that shall ever be killed have now been killed because the avenging of their blood has now begun. The one exception is that of the two witnesses.

With the sounding of each successive trumpet, the wrath of God pours out upon the earth. And with the sounding of the fifth trumpet we see the spirit of antichrist - the beast, who has been prophesied to come, ascend out of the bottomless pit upon the earth.

Revelation 9:1 *And the fifth angel sounded, and I saw a star fall from heaven unto the earth: and to him was given the key of the bottomless pit.* ***2*** *And <u>he opened the bottomless pit</u>; and there arose a smoke out of the pit, as the smoke of a great furnace; and the sun and the air were darkened by reason of the smoke of the pit.* ***3*** *And there came out of the smoke locusts upon the earth: and unto them was given power, as the scorpions of the earth have power.* ***4*** *And it was commanded them that they should not hurt the grass of the earth, neither any green thing, neither any tree; but only those men which have not the seal of God in their foreheads.*

Regarding these demonic locusts we are told…

Revelation 9:9-10…*and the sound of their wings was as the sound of chariots of many horses running to battle. And they had tails like unto scorpions, and there were stings in their tails: and their power was to hurt men five months.*

Revelation 9:11 *And they had a king over them, which is <u>the angel of the bottomless pit</u>, whose name in the Hebrew tongue is Abaddon, but in the Greek tongue hath his name <u>Apollyon</u>.* **12** *One woe is past; and, behold, there come two woes more hereafter.*

The king of the demonic locusts is the fallen angelic beast Apollyon. This angelic beast shall ascend out of the bottomless pit and will totally dominate the inhabitants of the earth commanding his army of locust demons on missions of torture. Can you imagine what it would be like for one of these locust demons to show up in your bedroom one night and sting you?

How do you think you would sleep the following night? It is called tribulation insomnia. We are told…

Revelation 9:6 *And in those days shall men seek death, and shall not find it; and shall desire to die, and death shall flee from them.*

This is real. This is not a novel. It is time for us to take our end time novels and our Left Behind Series books and give them a toss. It is time to discard fantasy and teach the truth of scripture about the dreadful fate of those left behind. The time is short.

For all who are left behind after the rapture of the church it will be like being stuck with one foot in the grave and the other foot in hell. During tribulation, men will be walking on the earth as the living damned with no way of escape. They will be under strong delusion and will all be forcibly branded with the mark of the beast.

Chapter 17 Babylon the Great - The City

The fall of the great city Babylon is a central feature in the book of Revelation. Understanding the symbolic significance of the great city Babylon is a vital key to the recognition of this important signal that indicates the impending return of the King of Kings. The fall of the city Babylon occurs near and prior to the beginning of the tribulation period.

Being alert to the occurrence of signals is important. When driving, we all look carefully at traffic signals because we know that when the yellow light signals, a major change is occurring and we must take action. Being alert to events of spiritual significance is important. Many failed to see that Jesus was the Messiah. Their preconceived ideas of Messiah caused them to disregard and overlook the truth when Jesus the Messiah came in the flesh. The fall of the city Babylon is the beginning of sorrows and a signal of the impending tribulation to come upon the earth. Just as many people fail to notice other important signals, many will fail to recognize the significance of the fall of the great city Babylon. This section will study characteristics of the city Babylon so that this important signal will not be overlooked.

Revelation 18:21 And a mighty angel took up a stone like a great millstone, and cast it into the sea, saying, Thus with violence shall that great city Babylon be thrown down, and shall be found no more at all.

The city Babylon will be totally destroyed. Destruction shall occur by being thrown down… falling with violence.

Revelation 18:1 And after these things I saw another angel come down from heaven, having great power; and the earth was lightened with his glory. 2 And he cried mightily with a strong voice, saying, Babylon the great is fallen, is fallen,

The fall of the city Babylon is also seen in a different vision of the same event in chapter 14.

***Revelation 14:6** And I saw another angel fly in the midst of heaven, having the everlasting gospel to preach unto them that dwell on the earth, and to every nation, and kindred, and tongue, and people, **7** Saying with a loud voice, Fear God, and give glory to him; for the hour of his judgment is come: and worship him that made heaven, and earth, and the sea, and the fountains of waters. **8** And there followed another angel, saying, <u>Babylon is fallen, is fallen, that great city</u>...*

Revelation 14:8 and Revelation 18:2 are different visions of the same <u>event</u>. Revelation 16:17-19 also mentions this same event but at <u>a later time</u> when the fall of the city Babylon comes into remembrance before God. We must keep in mind that the book of Revelation consists of a series of visions some of which describe the same events. Also we must carefully note that these visions are NOT presented in a chronological order. This knowledge is important to our understanding of the book of Revelation.

***Revelation 16:17** And the seventh angel poured out his vial into the air; and there came a great voice out of the temple of heaven, from the throne, saying, It is done. **18** And there were voices, and thunders, and lightnings; and there was a great earthquake, such as was not since men were upon the earth, so mighty an earthquake, and so great. **19** And the great city was divided into three parts, and <u>the cities of the nations fell: and great Babylon came in remembrance before God</u>...*

Revelation 16:19 above mentions the fall of the city Babylon, but at a later time when the event comes into the <u>remembrance</u> of God. The actual event of the fall of the city Babylon is seen in seen later in the book of Revelation in chapter 18. The event is also mentioned in Revelation chapter 14.

Revelation chapters 14, 16, and 18 do not occur in chronological order. In Revelation 16:18 a great earthquake occurs. This is near the <u>end</u> of the tribulation period. As a result of this great earthquake the cities of all nations fall. At this time the fall of the great city Babylon came in remembrance before God. The fall of the great city Babylon occurs earlier, near and prior to the beginning of the tribulation period but is described later in the book of Revelation in chapter 18. Next, we must review detailed characteristics of the city Babylon.

Revelation 18:15 *The merchants of these things, which were made rich by her, shall stand afar off for the fear of her torment, weeping and wailing,* ***16*** *And saying, Alas, alas, that great city, that was clothed in fine linen, and purple, and scarlet, and decked with gold, and precious stones, and pearls!* ***17*** *For in one hour so great riches is come to nought. And every shipmaster, and all the company in ships, and sailors, and as many as trade by sea, stood afar off,* ***18*** *And cried when they saw the smoke of her burning, saying, What city is like unto this great city!* ***19*** *And they cast dust on their heads, and cried, weeping and wailing, saying, Alas, alas, that great city, wherein were made rich all that had ships in the sea by reason of her costliness! for in one hour is she made desolate.*

Babylon is a great city. In the space of one hour the city Babylon is made totally desolate. Characteristics of the great city Babylon.
- Revelation 18:11 tells us that the merchants of the earth shall weep and mourn.
- (The merchants of the earth mourn because it was the center of world trade.)
- Revelation 18:9 tells us that the kings of the earth shall lament when they see the smoke of her burning.
- Revelation 18:3 tells us that the merchants of the earth (the world traders) were waxed rich through the abundance of her delicacies.
- Revelation 18:10 tells us that in one hour is her judgment come.
- Revelation 18:17 and 18 tells us that as many as trade by sea stood afar off and cried when they saw the smoke of her burning.
- Revelation 18:19 tells us that in one hour is she made desolate.
- Revelation 18:23 tells us that her merchants were the great men of the earth.

The Babylon of Revelation 18 is a great city which falls crashing to the ground -- a great city of commerce and trade for the entire world. A city the merchants of the world looked up to and grieve over. It is a great center of trade for the world.

Revelation 18:23*…thy merchants were the great men of the earth.*

- Babylon was a city of <u>merchants</u>.
- It was a city of the greatest merchants of the <u>earth</u>.

Revelation 18:10&11*…Alas, alas that great city Babylon, that mighty city! For in one hour is thy judgment come. And the <u>merchants of the earth</u> shall weep and mourn over her…*

Revelation 18:17&18*…as many as <u>trade</u> by sea, stood afar off, And cried when they saw the smoke of her burning, saying What city is like unto this great city.*

- Babylon was a city that would be mourned by those who <u>trade</u>.
- This is because Babylon was the center for world trade.
- The city of Babylon was a <u>world trade center</u> that falls crashing to the ground in total destruction.

Revelation 18:1&2 *And after these things I saw another angel come down from heaven, having great power; and the earth was lightened with his glory. And he cried mightily with a strong voice, saying, Babylon the great is fallen, is fallen…*

The angel cries saying Babylon is <u>fallen</u>…is <u>fallen</u>…The city Babylon is said to fall twice because it does fall twice.
- First tower <u>one</u>.
- Then tower <u>two</u>.

The twin towers of the World Trade Center fell 9-11-01…

That DAY was known over the entire earth as the <u>day of the great slaughter when the towers fell,</u> The <u>DAY of the great slaughter when the</u>

towers fell was prophesied by Isaiah to be seen on the earth just prior to the day of God's wrath pouring out upon the earth.

- It was a sign of the earth of blood, and fire, and vapour of smoke.
- It was a signal on the earth that the great day of the Lord is soon to come.
- It was a warning that the great tribulation is about to come upon the earth.

The following scriptures also describe the fall of the towering city followed closely by resurrection, rapture, and tribulation on the earth.

Isaiah 26:5 For he bringeth down them that dwell on high: the lofty city, he layeth it low; even to the ground; he bringeth it even to the dust.

Later in the same chapter…

Isaiah 26:19-21 Thy dead men shall live together with my dead body, shall they arise. Awake and sing, ye that dwell in dust: for thy dew is as the dew of herbs, and the earth shall cast out the dead. Come my people, enter thou into thy chambers, and shut thy doors about thee; hide thyself as it were for a little moment, until the indignation be overpast. For, behold, the Lord cometh out of his place to punish the inhabitants of the earth for their iniquity: the earth also shall disclose her blood, and shall no more cover her slain.

King of Babylon – AKA King of Tyrus

In the following passages note that the "king of Babylon" is Lucifer and that he is also referred to as "king of Tyrus." Also note that the city of Tyre is a symbolic name for the center of world trade.

*Ezekiel 28:12 Son of man, take up a lamentation upon the **king of Tyrus**, and say unto him, Thus saith the Lord GOD; Thou sealest up the sum, full of wisdom, and perfect in beauty. 13 Thou hast been in Eden* the garden of God; every precious stone was thy covering, the sardius, topaz, and the diamond, the beryl, the onyx, and the jasper, the sapphire, the emerald, and the carbuncle, and gold: the workmanship of thy tabrets and of thy pipes was prepared in thee in the day that thou wast created. **14** *Thou art the anointed cherub that covereth; and I have set thee so: thou wast upon the holy mountain of God; thou hast walked up and down in the midst of the stones of fire.* **15** *Thou wast perfect in thy ways from the day that thou wast created, till iniquity was found in thee.*

Lucifer is the king of Tyrus in the above passage, Tyrus is the symbolic name of the city which is the center of world trade.

- **Ezekiel 26:4** *And they shall destroy the walls of Tyrus, and break down her towers.*
- **Ezekiel 26:9** *And he shall set engines of war against thy walls, and with his axes he shall break down thy towers.*
- **Ezekiel 27:2-3** *Now, thou son of man, take up a lamentation for Tyrus; And say unto Tyrus, O thou that art situate at the entry of the sea, which art a <u>merchant of the people for many isles</u>, Thus saith the Lord God; O Tyrus, thou hast said, I am of perfect beauty.*
- **Ezekiel 27:11**..., *and the Gammadims were in thy towers...*
- **Ezekiel 27:12** *Tarshish was thy merchant by reason of the multitude of all kind of riches; with silver, iron, tin, and lead, they traded in thy fairs.*

In the next verse Ezekiel prophesies the fall of this towering center of world trade and this event would trigger astonishment and terror across the earth.

Ezekiel 27:34-35...<u>*thy merchandise*</u> *and all thy company in the midst of thee <u>shall fall.</u> All the inhabitants of the isles shall be astonished at thee, and their kings shall be sore afraid.*

Isaiah reveals another vision of the same events with the fall of a towering world trade center followed quickly by the great tribulation poured out upon the earth in Isaiah chapter 23 & 24.

- *Isaiah 23:1 The burden of Tyre, Howl, ye ships of tarshish; for it is laid waste...*
- *Isaiah 23:3...she is a <u>mart of nations.</u>*
- *Isaiah 23:8-9 Who hath taken this counsel against Tyre, the crowning city, whose merchants are princes, whose traffickers, are the honourable of the earth? The Lord of hosts hath purposed it, to stain the pride of all glory, and to bring into contempt all the honourable of the earth.*
- The crowning city is the <u>tallest</u> on earth.
- Traffickers of the earth are world <u>traders</u>.
- *Isaiah 23:11 He stretched out his hand over the sea, he shook the kingdoms: the Lord hath given a commandment against the merchant city, to destroy...*

The city of Tyre is a symbolic name for the center of world trade. After Tyre is destroyed come the judgments of tribulation upon the earth.

Isaiah 24:1 Behold, the Lord maketh the earth <u>empty</u>, and maketh it waste, and turneth it upside down, and scattereth abroad the inhabitants thereof.

Isaiah 24:20-21 The earth shall reel to and fro like a drunkard, and shall be removed like a cottage; and the transgression thereof shall be heavy upon it; and it shall fall, and not rise again. And it shall come to pass in that day, that the Lord shall punish the host of the high ones that are on high, and the kings of the earth upon the earth.

From a prophetic perspective, the fall of the World Trade Center was more than just a sign to signal the impending tribulation period. On 9-11-01 demonic spirits acting through demonized men had free reign to bring destruction to the World Trade Center. The fall of the World Trade Center was a foretaste of the tribulation period itself when demonic spirits will be given free reign not just at ground zero but over the entire earth.

Chapter 18 Mystery Babylon - A Fallen Angel

Revelation 17:1 And there came one of the seven angels which had the seven vials, and talked with me, saying unto me, Come hither; I will shew unto thee the <u>judgment of the great whore</u> that sitteth upon many waters: 2 With whom the kings of the earth have committed fornication, and the inhabitants of the earth have been made drunk with the wine of her fornication. 3 So he carried me away in the spirit into the wilderness: and I saw <u>a woman sit upon a scarlet coloured beast</u>, full of names of blasphemy...

- The woman is sitting on a scarlet <u>beast</u>.
- The beast is a fallen <u>angel</u>.
- The identity of the beast is the angel named <u>Apollyon</u>.
- Who is this woman? The identity of the woman is a mystery.

Revelation 17:5 And upon her forehead was a name written, MYSTERY, BABYLON THE GREAT, THE MOTHER OF HARLOTS AND ABOMINATIONS OF THE EARTH. 6 And I saw the woman drunken with the blood of the saints, and with the blood of the martyrs of Jesus:

- The woman has a name on her forehead. The name is a mystery.
- The name written on her forehead is <u>BABYLON</u> THE GREAT...
- She is the mother or one responsible for the <u>ABOMINATIONS</u> of the earth.
- She is the one responsible for the <u>blood</u> of the saints & the martyrs.
- The identity of the woman is a mystery.
- Who is this woman?
- The clue and solution to this mystery are found in the following verses in the book of Revelation.

Revelation 18:23...for by thy sorceries were <u>all nations deceived</u>. 24 And in her was found the blood of prophets, and of saints, and of all that were slain upon the earth.

- She is the one responsible for all that were <u>slain</u> on the earth.
- She is the one responsible for deceiving <u>all</u> nations.
- The beast, Apollyon is a DESTROYER.
- The woman MYSTERY BABYLON is a <u>DECEIVER</u>.
- The identity of the woman is a mystery.
- Who is this woman?
- She is the DECEIVER.

Revelation 12:9 And the great dragon was cast out, that old serpent, called the Devil, and Satan, which <u>deceiveth the whole world</u>: he was cast out into the earth, and his angels were cast out with him.

Revelation 20:7 *And when the thousand years are expired,* <u>Satan</u> *shall be loosed out of his prison,* ***8*** *And shall go out to* <u>deceive the nations...</u>

- Satan is the deceiver of the <u>nations</u>.
- Satan deceiveth the whole <u>world</u>.
- The woman is responsible for deceiving <u>all</u> nations.
- The woman is <u>Satan</u>.
- *Mystery Babylon a fallen angel.*
- *The beast is the fallen angel Apollyon,* <u>*the Destroyer*</u>*.*
- Mystery Babylon is the fallen angel Satan <u>the Deceiver</u>.

The above clues are key as we look into the following scriptures.

Revelation 17:1 *And there came one of the seven angels which had the seven vials, and talked with me, saying unto me, Come hither; I will shew unto thee the judgment of the great whore that sitteth upon many waters:*

- The whore <u>sits</u> on many waters.
- What are these waters?

Revelation 17:15 *And he saith unto me, The waters which thou sawest, where the whore* <u>*sitteth*</u>*, are peoples, and multitudes, and nations, and tongues.*

- To sit upon or over means to preside or reign over.
- Satan is called the "god of this world" and reigns over peoples, and multitudes, and nations, and tongues.

2 Corinthians 4:3&4 But if our gospel be hid, it is hid to them that are lost: In whom the <u>god of this world</u> hath blinded the minds of them which believe not…

- To blind the mind is to <u>deceive</u>.
- Satan is the <u>DECEIVER</u>.

Revelation 17:1 And there came one of the seven angels which had the seven vials, and talked with me, saying unto me, Come hither; I will shew unto thee the judgment of the great whore that sitteth upon many waters: 2 With whom the kings of the earth have committed fornication, and the inhabitants of the earth have been made drunk with the wine of her fornication. 3 So he carried me away in the spirit into the wilderness: and I saw a woman sit upon a scarlet coloured beast, full of names of blasphemy, having <u>seven heads and ten horns</u>.

What are the seven heads and the ten horns? Let's look at another example of seven heads and ten horns from Revelation chapter 12.

Revelation 12:3 And there appeared another wonder in heaven; and behold a great red dragon, having <u>seven heads and ten horns,</u> and seven crowns upon his heads. 4 And his tail drew the third part of the stars of heaven, and did cast them to the earth:

In this case rather than the beast it is the dragon Satan who has seven heads and ten horns. The beast is the fallen angel Apollyon. The dragon is the fallen angel Satan.

The vision of the seven heads and ten horns is a vision of the makeup of the kingdom of darkness, a vision of that with which we wrestle. The heads and horns represent principalities and rulers in the kingdom of darkness. The following scriptures define details of this important symbolism. What do horns symbolize?

Revelation 5:6 *And I beheld, and, lo, in the midst of the throne and of the four beasts, and in the midst of the elders, stood a Lamb as it had been slain, having seven <u>horns</u> and seven eyes, which are the seven <u>Spirits</u> of God sent forth into all the earth.*

Horns symbolize spirits. What do heads symbolize?

Revelation 17:9 *And here is the mind which hath wisdom. The <u>seven heads are seven mountains</u>, <u>on which the woman sitteth</u>.*

Heads symbolize <u>mountains</u>. Mountains are high places... principalities in the kingdom of darkness. The term "mountain" signifies <u>kingdom</u>. "Mountain" also in this sense carries a meaning of authority or rulership. A mountain is a kingdom or a principality. A principality is a segment of a kingdom over which a prince rules. The kingdom of darkness is divided into seven major principalities. These seven principalities are the mountains on which the woman sits... presides and reigns over.

The next two scriptures are examples of the use of the word "mount" or "mountain" to represent <u>kingdom and rulership</u>.

Isaiah 14:12 *How art thou fallen from heaven, O Lucifer, son of the morning! how art thou cut down to the ground, which didst weaken the nations!* **13** *For thou hast said in thine heart, I will ascend into heaven, I will exalt my throne above the stars of God: I will **sit also upon the mount** of the congregation, in the sides of the north:* **14** *I will ascend above the heights of the clouds; I will be like the most High.* **15** *Yet thou shalt be brought down to hell, to the sides of the pit.*

Ezekiel 28:14 *Thou art the anointed cherub that covereth; and I have set thee so: thou wast upon the **holy mountain of God**; thou hast walked up and down in the midst of the stones of fire.* **15** *Thou wast* *perfect in thy ways from the day that thou wast created, till iniquity was found in thee. By the multitude of thy merchandise they have filled the midst of thee with violence, and thou hast sinned: therefore I will cast thee as profane out of the <u>mountain of God</u>: and I will destroy thee, O covering cherub*

- The mountain of God is the Kingdom of God.
- Mountains also symbolize principalities in the kingdom of darkness.
- These mountains are heads in the visions of Revelation 12:3, and 17:3.

Satan in rebellion attempted to sit upon or reign over the mountain of God in heaven, thus was cast out. The woman Satan now sits on or reigns over the seven principalities or <u>mountains</u> in the kingdom of darkness. The vision of the seven heads and ten horns symbolizes the principalities and ruler spirits that make up the kingdom of darkness with which we wrestle.

Ephesians 5:12 *For we wrestle not against flesh and blood, but against <u>principalities</u>, against powers, against the <u>rulers</u> of the darkness of this world, against spiritual wickedness in <u>high places</u>.*

Revelation 17:9 *And here is the mind which hath wisdom. The seven heads are seven mountains, <u>on which the woman sitteth</u>.*

There are also princes or rulers in the kingdom of darkness over each principality. Each of these rulers is called a king. These are not human kings, they are demonic kings... fallen angels... spirits...rulers in the kingdom of darkness.

Revelation 17:1 *And there came one of the seven angels which had the seven vials, and talked with me, saying unto me, Come hither; I will shew unto thee the <u>judgment of the great whore that **sitteth** upon many waters</u>: 2 With whom the kings of the earth have committed fornication,* *and the inhabitants of the earth have been made drunk with the wine of her fornication. 3 So he carried me away in the spirit into the wilderness: and I saw a woman sit upon a scarlet coloured beast, full of names of blasphemy, <u>having seven heads and ten horns</u>. 4 And the woman was arrayed in purple and scarlet colour, and decked with gold and precious stones and pearls, having a golden cup in her hand full of abominations and filthiness of her fornication: 5 And upon her forehead was a name written, MYSTERY, BABYLON THE GREAT, THE MOTHER OF HARLOTS AND ABOMINATIONS OF THE EARTH. 6 And I saw the woman drunken with the blood of the saints, and with the blood of the martyrs of Jesus: and when I saw her, I wondered with great admiration. 7 And the angel said unto me, Wherefore didst thou marvel? I will tell thee the mystery of the woman, and of the beast that carrieth her, which hath the seven heads and ten horns. 8 The beast that thou sawest <u>was, and is not; and shall ascend out of the bottomless pit, and go into perdition</u>: and they that dwell on the earth shall wonder, whose names were not written in the book of life from the foundation of the world, when they behold the beast that was, and is not, and yet is.*

Revelation 17:8 The beast that thou sawest <u>was</u>, and <u>is not</u>; and <u>shall ascend out of the bottomless pit, and go into perdition</u>:

Those dwelling on the earth will be those whose names are not written in the lambs book of life. The unusual appearance of this angelic beast will cause them to wonder when they <u>behold</u> the beast that <u>was, and is not, and yet is</u>.

- The beast **was** at the throne of God.
- The beast **is not** because he is concealed in the bottomless pit.
- The beast shall <u>ascend</u> out of the bottomless pit.
- The beast shall go into <u>perdition</u>. Perdition means destruction.

Destruction of the beast will occur in…

Revelation 19:20 *And the beast was taken, and with him the false prophet that wrought miracles before him, with which he deceived them that had received the mark of the beast, and them that worshipped his image. These both were <u>cast alive into a lake of fire</u> burning with brimstone.*

Now continuing in chapter 17…

Revelation 17:9 *And here is the mind which hath wisdom. The seven heads are seven mountains, on which the woman sitteth.* **10** *And there are seven kings: five are fallen, and one is, and the other is not yet come; and when he cometh, he must continue a short space.* **11** *And the beast that was, <u>and is not</u>, even he is the eighth, and is of the seven, and goeth into perdition.*

- The beast that was, and is not, even he is the eighth <u>king</u>.
- The beast is also one of the seven <u>kings</u>.
- The beast is an <u>angel</u>, a spirit ruler in the kingdom of darkness.
- Like the beast, the other kings are also <u>angels</u>, spirit rulers in that kingdom.
- The beast is the one of the seven kings who has not yet <u>come</u>.
- The beast is that spirit of antichrist who has been prophesied to <u>come</u>.

Revelation 17:10 *…the other is not yet come; and when he cometh, he must continue a short space.*

The beast has not yet come upon the earth. When he comes he will reign a short space of only 42 months or 3 and ½ years as seen in Revelation 13:5. This short space shall be the entirety of the tribulation period.

Revelation 17:9 *And here is the mind which hath wisdom. The seven heads are seven mountains, on which the woman sitteth.* **10** *And there* *are seven kings: five are fallen, and <u>one is</u>, and the other is not yet come…*

Of the seven kings, Satan is the one that *"<u>is</u>."* Satan presides or reigns over all the other rulers in the kingdom of darkness. Satan sits on all seven mountains which represent the seven major principalities in his kingdom. The other five kings are fallen angels. Satan is also a fallen angel, but he still *"<u>is</u>"* in the sense that he has had access to the throne of God in heaven to accuse the brethren.

The beast "<u>was, and is not</u>" because he was at the throne, but now "<u>is not</u>," being locked in the bottomless pit. Satan's continued access to the throne to accuse the brethren came about through the fall of man, and man's relinquishment of authority over to Satan.

Revelation 17:12 *And the ten horns which thou sawest are ten kings…*

Do you remember what horns symbolize? Horns symbolize <u>spirits</u>.

Revelation 17:12 *And the ten horns which thou sawest are ten kings, which have received no kingdom as yet; but receive power as kings one hour with the beast.* ***13*** *These have one mind, and shall give their power and strength unto the beast.*

- These ten kings are not human kings.
- The ten kings are <u>spirits</u> in the kingdom of darkness.
- The ten kings are fallen <u>angels</u>.
- They are rulers over <u>principalities</u> and powers in the kingdom of darkness.
- The ten kings are of one accord. They are of <u>one</u> mind.
- To give their <u>power</u> unto the beast.

Why do the ten kings want to give their power to the beast? They are about to help the beast wage two wars. The second of these two wars <u>will be their final war</u> because it is against the King of Kings and the Lord of Lords, Jesus Christ. The specifics of this war are revealed in the following two scriptures…

Revelation 17:12 *And the ten horns which thou sawest are ten kings, which have received no kingdom as yet; but receive power as kings one hour with the beast.* ***13*** *These have one mind, and shall give their power and strength unto the beast.* ***14*** *These shall make war with the Lamb, and the Lamb shall overcome them: for he is Lord of lords, and King of kings: and they that are with him are called, and chosen, and faithful.*

Revelation 19:19 *And I saw the beast, and the kings of the earth, and their armies, gathered together to make war against him that sat on the horse, and against his army.* ***20*** *And the beast was taken, and with him the false prophet that wrought miracles before him, with which he deceived them that had received the mark of the beast, and them that worshipped his image. These both were cast alive into a lake of fire burning with brimstone.*

The ten kings who give their power to the beast are called the kings of the <u>earth</u>. When they all go to war against Jesus they all wind up in the lake of <u>fire</u>. But prior to this, the beast and the ten kings will wage a different war. This war is for control of the kingdom of darkness.

It is a coup in the kingdom of darkness.

Revelation 17:16 *And the ten horns which thou sawest upon the beast, these shall hate the whore, and shall make her desolate and naked, and shall eat her flesh, and burn her with fire.* ***17*** *For God hath put in their hearts to fulfil his will, and **to agree**, and give their kingdom unto the beast...*

The ten horns are fallen <u>angels</u> who hate the whore, Satan. *Why?* Satan <u>deceived</u> them to rebel and be cast out of heaven. They attack the whore because God put it into their hearts to fulfil his will, and to <u>agree</u>, and give their kingdom unto the beast. Their kingdom is the kingdom of darkness. Through this attack, the throne of the kingdom of darkness is taken from Satan and given unto the beast.

- The kingdom of the ten kings is the kingdom of darkness.
- Through this attack the ten kings give their kingdom unto the beast.
- Reign of the kingdom of darkness is taken from Satan.
- Reign of the kingdom of darkness is given over to the beast.

The judgment of the whore is Satan's loss of rulership over his kingdom which is given over to the beast.

Revelation 17:1 *And there came one of the seven angels which had the seven vials, and talked with me, saying unto me, Come hither; I will shew unto thee the judgment of the great whore that sitteth upon many waters:*

But the ultimate judgment of Satan, the beast, and all their company will be the lake of fire.

Revelation 17:16 *And the ten horns which thou sawest upon the beast, these shall hate the whore, and shall make her desolate and naked, and shall eat her flesh, and burn her with fire.* ***17*** *For God hath put in their hearts to fulfil his will, and to agree, and give their kingdom unto the beast, until the words of God shall be fulfilled.* ***18*** *And the woman which thou sawest is that great city, which reigneth over the kings of the earth.*

The woman is Satan who reigns over the kings of the earth… over the other rulers in the kingdom of darkness. *But why is the woman, Satan, called a city?*

Strong's definitions:
- Babel – confusion Babel (i.e. Babylon)   Strongs #894
- Lucifer -Title applied to king of Babylon.
- Babylon means "babel," as in the tower of Babel.
- The city Babylon was a city of towers.

The city Babylon was a re-enactment of the tower of babel, this time built as a set of twin towers reaching into the heavens to "make a name" for or exalt the world financial system. And <u>Lucifer</u> is the title applied to the <u>king of Babylon</u>.

Genesis 11:4 *(re: building the tower of Babel) And they said, Go to, let us build us a city and a tower, whose top may reach unto heaven; and let us <u>make us a name</u>…*

The great city Babylon was a re-enactment of the <u>tower of Babel</u>. These towers were built to be the tallest and most impressive towers on the face of the earth to "*<u>make a name</u>*" for or to exalt the prestige of the world financial system.

The city Babylon was the center of world trade and the pinnacle of the world financial system. Lucifer is the title applied to the king of Babylon and therefore the king over this city. The world financial system is a major principality in Satan's kingdom of darkness. Why? *The love of money is the root of all evil…* **1 *Timothy* 6:10**

This city of towers represented, in the spiritual realm, an idol on the face of the earth. The ruler of the kingdom of darkness desires to have an idol or image erected upon the face of the earth to signify worship to him.

Satan is the <u>deceiver</u>. He deceived men into building the tallest towers on earth to exalt the world financial system and to be a re-enactment of the tower of Babel and an idol unto him. The men who built theses towers didn't even know what they were doing. They were <u>deceived</u>.

But the beast Apollyon is the <u>destroyer</u>. People under the rule of the beast will be <u>forced</u> to build an image or idol on the face of the earth to glorify him. These people will know what they are doing, and if they don't built it and worship it <u>they will be killed</u>, they will be <u>destroyed</u>.

***Revelation* 13:14** *And deceiveth them that dwell on the earth by the means of those miracles which he had power to do in the sight of the beast; saying to them that dwell on the earth, that they should make an image to the beast…*

***Revelation* 13:15** *And he had power to give life unto the image of the* *beast, that the image of the beast should both speak, and cause that as many as would not worship the image of the beast should be killed.*

The spirit Mystery Babylon and the city Babylon are intimately connected. The fall of the idol towers signifies the impending end of the reign of Satan, the spirit behind the idol. The fall of the towers of Babylon will be followed by man's erecting the image of the beast upon the face of the earth. This structure will signify the beasts reign over the inhabitants of the earth.

The fall of the city Babylon is a sign on the earth of the impending rapture of the church, and the impending tribulation period. It is a sign of the impending ascension of the fallen angelic beast out of the bottomless pit, and of the beast's impending ascension to the seat of rulership over the kingdom of darkness.

Satan's loss of supremacy over the kingdom of darkness and the destruction of his idol towers constitute the judgment of the whore. (Revelation 17:1) The ultimate judgment for Satan and the beast Apollyon, will be the lake of fire.

Chapter 19 The Abomination of Desolation

Matthew 24:14 *And of this gospel of the Kingdom shall be preached in all the world for a witness unto all nations; and then shall the end come.* ***15*** *When ye therefore shall see the ABOMINATION OF DESOLATION, spoken of by Daniel the prophet, stand in the <u>holy place</u>, (whoso readeth, let him understand:)* ***16*** *Then let them which be in Ju-dae-a flee into the mountains:* ***17*** *Let him which is upon the housetop not come down to take anything out of his house:* ***18*** *Neither let him which is in the field return back to take his clothes.* ***19*** *And woe unto them that are with child, and to them that give suck in those days!* ***20*** *But pray ye that your flight be not in the winter, neither on the sabbath day:* ***21*** *For then shall be great <u>tribulation</u>, such as was not since the beginning of the world to this time, no, nor ever shall be.*

- The ABOMINATION OF DESOLATION is spoken of by <u>Daniel</u> the prophet,
- It will stand or occur in the <u>holy</u> place,
- The holy place is on the <u>temple</u> mount in Jerusalem.
- Those who are in Ju-dae-a are instructed to flee into the <u>mountains</u> when they see the <u>Abomination of Desolation</u>.
- These are the people of the nation of <u>Israel</u>.
- They are to evacuate into the mountains with haste.
- This will be the beginning of great <u>tribulation</u> on the earth.

Why does Jesus tell Israel to flee to the mountains? Where are they to go then?

Revelation 12:3 *And there appeared another wonder in heaven; and behold a great red dragon, having seven heads and ten horns, and seven crowns upon his heads.* ***4*** *And his tail drew the third part of the stars of heaven, and did cast them to the earth: and the dragon stood before the woman which was ready to be delivered, for to devour her child as soon as it was born.* ***5*** *And she brought forth a man child, who was to rule all nations with a rod of iron: and her child was caught up unto God, and to his throne.* ***6*** *And the woman fled into the wilderness, where she hath <u>a</u>*

place prepared of God, *that they should feed her there a thousand two hundred and threescore days.*

- The dragon is <u>Satan</u>.
- The woman is <u>Israel</u>.
- The man child the woman brings forth is <u>Jesus</u>.
- Jesus will rule all nations with a <u>rod</u> of iron.
- Jesus has been caught up to God and to his <u>throne</u>.
- Jesus is at the right hand of the <u>Father</u> at the throne.

Beginning again at verse 5…

Revelation 12:5 *And she brought forth a man child, who was to rule all nations with a rod of iron: and her child was caught up unto God, and to his throne* **6** *And the woman **fled** into the wilderness, where she hath <u>a place prepared of God</u>, that they should <u>feed her</u> there <u>a thousand two hundred and threescore</u> **days**.*

- In the vision, the woman (Israel) <u>fled</u> into the wilderness.
- Jesus tells Israel to flee to the <u>mountains</u> in Matthew chapter 24.
- Jesus tells Israel to flee to the wilderness because there will be a place <u>prepared</u> of God.
- God will feed Israel in the wilderness 1260 days or <u>3 ½ years</u>.

Revelation 12:14 *And to the woman were given two wings of a great eagle, that she might fly into the wilderness, into her place, where <u>she is nourished</u> for a time, and times, and half a time, from the face of the serpent.*

In the wilderness Israel will be nourished. They will be fed the Word of God as they see Jesus as their Messiah. The Lord will <u>confirm the holy covenant</u> of His blood with Israel in the wilderness for 1260 days (3 ½ years.)

Zechariah 12:10 *And I will pour upon the house of David, and upon the inhabitants of Jerusalem, the spirit of grace and of supplications: <u>and they shall look upon me whom they have pierced, and they shall mourn</u>*

for him, *as one mourneth for his only son, and shall be in bitterness for him, as one that is in bitterness for his first born.*

Zechariah 13:1 *In that day there shall be a fountain opened to the house of David and to the inhabitants of Jerusalem for sin and for uncleaness.*

The 1260 days or 3 and ½ years that Israel is fed in the wilderness will be the second half of the 70th week of Daniel. Daniel 9:27 states that he (meaning the Messiah) will confirm the covenant with many for one week (or seven years.) The first half of that 70th week was the 3 and ½ year ministry of Jesus to Israel that took place prior to his death on the cross. At the midpoint of that 70th week He, the Messiah, took away the sacrifice and caused it to cease as seen in Daniel 9:27 and also seen in Hebrews 10:9.

The abomination of desolation is spoken of by Daniel. The book of Daniel gives precise information of the timing of end time events. But to understand these end time prophecies we must understand precisely and exactly what the abomination of desolation is.

Matthew 24:15 *When ye therefore shall see the abomination of desolation, spoken of by Daniel the prophet, stand in the holy place, (whoso readeth, let him understand:)* **16** *Then let them which be in Judaea flee into the mountains:*

What will those who are to flee to the mountains actually see happen on the temple mount on the site of the holy place? Why will they flee?

The prototype of the abomination of desolation was when the ancient king Antiochus Epiphanes conquered Jerusalem. This king, who hated Israel, went into the holy place set up an idol to Zeus and sacrificed the blood of the biggest ugliest pig he could find. This sacrifice was an affront to the God of Israel. The blood of the pig was an unacceptable blood sacrifice. This unacceptable blood sacrifice in the holy place was known as the abomination of desolation.

The abomination of desolation is an <u>unacceptable blood sacrifice</u> offered to God in the holy place. But in what manner could there be an <u>unacceptable blood sacrifice</u> offered to God in our time? The answer to this question lies in the *mystery of the red heifer* which shall be solved in the appendix section of this book on pages 214 – 216.

Hebrews 10:6-9 *IN BURNT OFFERINGS AND SACRIFICES FOR SIN THOU HAST HAD NO PLEASURE. THEN SAID I, LO, I COME (IN THE VOLUME OF THE BOOK IT IS WRITTEN OF ME,) TO DO THY WILL, O GOD. Above when he said, Sacrifice and offering and burnt offerings and offering for sin thou wouldest not, neither hadst pleasure therein; which are offered by law; Then said he, Lo, I come to do thy will, O God.* <u>*He taketh away the first, that he may establish the second.*</u>

Hebrews 10:10 *By the which will we are sanctified through the offering of the body of Jesus Christ once for all.*

- Jesus came to do the will of God and <u>take away the first</u> system of sacrifice.
- Jesus the Messiah took away the first sacrifice causing it to <u>cease</u>.
- Jesus the Messiah took away the <u>first sacrifice</u> that He may establish the <u>second</u>.
- By which we are sanctified through the offering of the body of <u>Jesus Christ</u>.
- This happened <u>once for all</u>. That by the perfect will of God there should be <u>no further sacrifices</u>.

Hebrews 10:14 *For by one offering he hath perfected for ever them that are sanctified. 15 Whereof the Holy Ghost also is a witness to us: for after that he had said before, 16 This is the covenant that I will make with them after those days, saith the Lord, I will put my laws into their hearts, and in their minds will I write them; 17 And their sins and iniquities will I remember no more. 18 Now where remission of these is,* <u>*there is no more offering for sin.*</u>

What if someone continued to offer the blood of an animal to try to obtain forgiveness of sins? They will find that there is no more offering for sin by the sacrifice of the blood of an animal. The blood of an animal is no longer an acceptable sacrifice for sins.

Hebrews 10:26 *For if we sin wilfully after that we have received the knowledge of the truth,* <u>*there remaineth no more sacrifice for sins*</u>*,*

The willful sin to be avoided in verse 26 above is a <u>very specific sin</u> which is the continued offering of the blood sacrifice of an animal by someone who does not trust in the blood of Jesus for their complete forgiveness of sins. This is the theme of Hebrews chapter 10. This was written to the Hebrews to warn them against turning back to the law and animal sacrifices. The willful sin of offering the blood sacrifice of an animal according to the law will in no way atone for sin. <u>There remains no more sacrifice for sins by the blood of an animal</u>.

All sin is totally forgiven by the blood of Jesus by which Hebrews 10:14 explains that we have been made forever perfect. Sin cannot be forgiven by the blood of an animal. Those who commit the sin of trying to trust in the blood of an animal for the forgiveness of sins will find that <u>there remaineth no more sacrifice for sins</u> as described in the following verse.

Hebrews 10:26 *For if we sin wilfully after that we have received the knowledge of the truth,* <u>*there remaineth no more sacrifice for sins*</u>*,...*

Hebrews 10:29 *Of how much sorer punishment, suppose ye, shall he be thought worthy, who hath trodden underfoot the Son of God, and hath counted the* <u>*blood of the covenant*</u>*, wherewith he was sanctified, an unholy thing, and hath done despite unto the Spirit of grace.*

The offering of the blood of an animal as a sacrifice would be counting the <u>blood of the covenant</u> an unholy thing and something done despite unto, as an insult to the Spirit of grace. The offering of the blood of an animal would be an <u>unacceptable sacrifice</u>, an abomination.

The offering of the blood of an animal will be the enactment of the ABOMINATION OF DESOLATION and will be the initiation of the great tribulation period on the earth. Even now Jews are preparing to make just such an animal sacrifice. This animal sacrifice will be made out of a spirit of <u>antichrist</u>.

1 John 4:3 And <u>every spirit</u> that confesseth not that Jesus Christ is come in the flesh is not of God: and this is that <u>spirit of antichrist</u>, whereof ye have heard that <u>it should come</u>; and even now already is in the world.

1 John 2:18 Little children, it is the last time: and as ye have heard that <u>antichrist shall come</u>, even now are there many antichrists; whereby we know that it is the last time.

When John wrote the above scripture there were many antichrist spirits, but there is also an antichrist spirit who shall come. The Jews who make this animal sacrifice will do so out of a <u>spirit of antichrist</u>. If they confessed that Jesus the Messiah had come in the flesh, they would not be offering animal sacrifice for sin according to the law. Thus they will be operating under a spirit of antichrist.

This animal sacrifice will be done out of a spirit of antichrist who is already on the earth. And this ABOMINATION OF DESOLATION will directly lead to the events of the day of the Lord and the release of an even more powerful spirit of antichrist who has been prophesied to come. This will be the release of the beast Apollyon, the angel that shall ascend out of the bottomless pit.

The sacrifice of the blood of Jesus offered on the cross was the initiation of the outpouring of grace upon the earth. The unacceptable blood sacrifice of an animal offered in the holy place, the abomination of desolation, will be the initiation of the outpouring of the wrath of God upon the earth.

When the blood of Jesus was shed on the cross there were several immediate manifestations on the earth. (See Luke 23:44-45)

Three of these manifestations were...
- <u>earthquake,</u>
- <u>total darkness,</u>
- <u>resurrection of the dead.</u> (See Luke 23:44-45)

The sacrifice of the blood of an animal will be an unacceptable blood. When the blood of the animal is shed and this abomination of desolation takes place there will be evident the following immediate manifestations ...
- <u>earthquake,</u>
- <u>total darkness,</u>
- <u>resurrection of the dead.</u>

The manifestations of earthquake, total darkness, and resurrection of the dead who are in Christ shall occur on the great and notable day of the Lord. The resurrection of the dead on that day will immediately precede the rapture of the church as described in the following passage from 1 Thessalonians chapter 4. These events will occur on the DAY OF THE LORD as noted as the passage continues with the very next verse in chapter 5.

*1Thessalonians 4:15 For this we say unto you by the word of the Lord, that we which are alive and remain unto the coming of the Lord shall not prevent them which are asleep. **16** For the Lord himself shall descend from heaven with a shout, with the voice of the archangel, and with the trump of God: and the dead in Christ shall rise first: **17** <u>Then we which are alive and remain shall be caught up together with them in the clouds</u>, to meet the Lord in the air: and so shall we ever be with the Lord. **18** Wherefore comfort one another with these words:* **Chapter 5:1** *But of the times and the seasons, brethren, ye have no need that I write unto you. **2** For yourselves know perfectly that* **the day of the Lord** *so cometh as a thief in the night.*

NOTE CAREFULLY: IMPORTANT KEY DETAIL - The above passage clearly identifies this fact…THE <u>RAPTURE</u> OF THE CHURCH OCCURS ON <u>THE DAY OF THE LORD</u>.

The sacrifice of the blood of Jesus once and for all took away the blood sacrifice of an animal offered for sin according to the law. The abomination of desolation will be the blood sacrifice of an animal offered according to the law.

This blood sacrifice of an animal…
- will not be a blood sacrifice <u>for</u> sin,
- but will be a blood sacrifice <u>of</u> sin.

This blood sacrifice of an animal
- will not be a blood sacrifice that <u>covers</u> sin,
- but will be a blood sacrifice that <u>commits</u> sin.

This blood sacrifice of an animal will be an <u>abomination</u>. The abomination of desolation will be the blood sacrifice of an animal that will trigger the events of the DAY OF THE LORD.

How will this blood sacrifice of an animal take place? The answer is in the *mystery of the red heifer* as detailed in the appendix of this book on pages 214 - 216.

Chapter 20 Left Behind - The Teaching of Jesus

Novels and fantasies have been devised describing the fate of those "Left Behind" after the rapture of the Church. This chapter will focus on what Jesus taught about the actual fate of all those who are left behind.

In Luke chapter 21 Jesus is speaking of the day of the Lord that *"shall come as a snare upon all them that dwell on the face of the whole earth. "* Who then can be saved from this all encompassing snare? The answer is found only in escape. You must not be left behind dwelling upon the earth, you must escape. That escape is commonly referred to as the rapture of the Church.

Luke 21:35-36 *For as a snare shall <u>it</u> come on all them that dwell on the face of the whole earth. Watch ye therefore, and pray always, that ye may be accounted worthy to* **<u>escape</u>** *all these things that shall come to pass, and* **<u>to stand before the Son of man.</u>**

The Strong's definition for the word "escape" means to "seek safety in flight." After the rapture of the Church those left behind dwelling on the earth shall be caught in a snare. They shall not escape.

The phrase "<u>escape to</u>" defines <u>where</u> they are to go. The church escapes in flight <u>to stand before the Son of man</u>. Jesus, the Son of man, is at the right hand of the Father at the throne in Heaven.

Those who escape in flight, the rapture of the Church, will be standing before the throne in heaven. All those who do not escape in the rapture will be left behind. They shall not escape. The words, <u>escape… to stand before the Son of man,</u> describes the rapture of the church and is a reference also seen in the vision of the rapture seen in Revelation chapter 7 verse 9 .

Revelation 7:9 *After this I beheld, and, lo, a great multitude, which no man could number, of all nations, and kindreds, and people, and tongues, <u>stood</u> before the throne, and <u>before the Lamb</u>, clothed with white robes, and palms in their hands;*

Jesus said that we are to watch and pray that we may be <u>accounted</u> worthy to escape. None are worthy by their own righteousness. We are accounted worthy by one thing only, the blood of Jesus Christ.

It shall come to pass on the day of the Lord that whosoever shall call on the name of the Lord Jesus shall be saved. They shall escape in the rapture of the Church and will stand before the Son of man in heaven. For those left behind it will be too late.

Jesus also taught that the elect would have to be evacuated to escape the deception of the beast in Mark chapter 13.

__Mark 13:22__ ...false prophets shall rise, and shall shew signs and wonders, to seduce, if it were possible, even the elect.

What will occur to make it not possible for the elect to be deceived? We see the soution to this mystery as the passage continues.

__Mark 13:26-27__ And then shall they see the Son of man coming in the clouds with great power and glory. And then shall he send his angels, and shall gather together his <u>elect</u>...

Which brings us to our next question. If the <u>elect</u> who have the Spirit of God must be evacuated to escape the deception and power of the beast, what chance does an unsaved person have who is left behind? The answer is none. There will be no hope for those left behind. Perhaps the most important teaching on the dreadful fate of all those left behind is powerfully presented by Jesus Christ in the parable of the ten virgins.

__Matthew 25:1__ Then shall the kingdom of heaven be likened unto ten virgins, which took their lamps, and went forth to meet the bridegroom. __2__ And five of them were wise, and five were foolish. __3__ They that were foolish took their lamps, and took no oil with them: __4__ But the wise took oil in their vessels with their lamps. __5__ While the bridegroom tarried, they all slumbered and slept. __6__ And at midnight there was a cry made, Behold, *the bridegroom cometh; go ye out to meet him. 7 Then all those virgins arose, and trimmed their lamps. 8 And the foolish said unto the wise, Give us of your oil; for our lamps are gone out. 9 But the wise answered, saying, Not so; lest there be not enough for us and you: but go ye rather to them that sell, and buy for yourselves. 10 And while they went to buy, the bridegroom came; and they that were ready went in with him to the marriage: and the door was shut. 11 Afterward came also the other virgins, saying, Lord, Lord, open to us. 12 But he answered and said, Verily I say unto you, I know you not. 13 Watch therefore, for ye know neither the day nor the hour wherein the Son of man cometh.*

In the above passage verse 10 is speaking of the marriage of the Lamb and the rapture of the church. What does Jesus clearly teach about those left behind outside the door of the marriage chamber when He comes for his bride? After the wise virgins enter the marriage chamber with the groom the door is shut. This is a perfect picture of the rapture of the Church. Those left behind outside the door are knocking. They are seeking the Lord and calling on His name. But it is now too late.

The foolish virgins were left behind. They were seeking the Lord and calling on him. But they were seeking the Lord after it was too late.

Isaiah 55:6 *Seek ye the LORD while he may be found.*

The prophet Isaiah knew that a day was coming when the dispensation of grace would be over. He knew that a day would come when it would be too late to seek and find the Lord.

Jesus taught this in the parable of the ten virgins. Clearly, it will be too late for those left behind outside the door of the marriage chamber when He comes for his bride. To teach otherwise regarding those "left behind" is to teach a fantasy in contradiction to the direct teachings of our Lord Jesus Christ. Today is the day of salvation. You must not be left behind.

Chapter 21 Understanding the Seventy Weeks and the 3 & ½ year tribulation

Daniel 9:20 *And whiles I was speaking, and praying, and confessing my sin and the sin of my people Israel, and presenting my supplication before the LORD my God for the holy mountain of my God;* ***21*** *Yea, whiles I was speaking in prayer, even the man Gabriel, whom I had seen in the vision at the beginning, being caused to fly swiftly, touched me about the time of the evening oblation.* ***22*** *And he informed me, and talked with me, and said, O Daniel, I am now come forth to give thee skill and understanding.*

- Daniel was presenting supplication to the Lord for the holy mountain of God.
- The mountain of God is the kingdom of God.
- The man Gabriel touched Daniel and talked with him. Gabriel is an angel.
- Gabriel comes to Daniel to give him skill and understanding.
- Understanding of future events comes from the Lord.
- Understanding comes through the avenue of prayer.

Daniel 9:23 *At the beginning of thy supplications the commandment came forth, and I am come to shew thee; for thou art greatly beloved: therefore understand the matter, and consider the vision.* ***24*** *Seventy weeks are determined upon thy people and upon thy holy city, to finish the transgression, and to make an end of sins, and to make reconciliation for iniquity, and to bring in everlasting righteousness, and to seal up the vision and prophecy, and to anoint the most Holy.*

- Daniel is told by Gabriel to consider the vision.
- Seventy weeks are determined upon thy people.
- And upon thy holy city.
- The people of Daniel are the children of Israel.
- The holy city is the city of Jerusalem.
- The seventy weeks are determined on Israel and Jerusalem.
- Events in the gentile world will not be considered when counting the 70 weeks.

Daniel 9:24 *Seventy weeks are determined upon thy people and upon thy holy city, to finish the transgression, and to make an end of sins, and to make reconciliation for iniquity, and to bring in everlasting righteousness, and to seal up the vision and prophecy, and to anoint the most Holy.*

In Daniel's vision of the seventy weeks, each week actually represents a time period of seven years. All of the following events will be fulfilled during the 70 weeks of Daniel. *Seventy weeks are determined on the people of Israel and Jerusalem…*

- to finish transgression
- to make an end of sins
- to make reconciliation for iniquity
- to bring in everlasting righteousness
- to seal up the vision and the prophecy
- and to <u>anoint</u> the most Holy

The first of these important events to occur is the sealing of the vision and prophecy. This is accomplished as Daniel is told in Daniel chapter 12.

Daniel 12:4 *But thou, O Daniel, shut up the words, and seal the book, even to the time of the end…*

Next, reconciliation for iniquity, the finish of transgression, and the making of an end of sins were accomplished by Jesus on the cross at a point later in the timeline of Daniel's 70 weeks.

The first 69 weeks were prior to the ministry of the Messiah Jesus. At the beginning of the 70th week Jesus the most Holy, was <u>anointed</u> and His ministry began as seen in Mark 1:10.

Mark 1:10 *And it came to pass in those days, that Jesus came from Nazareth of Galilee, and was baptized of John in Jordan. And straightway coming up out of the water, he saw the heavens opened, and <u>the Spirit like a dove descending upon him</u>:*

The day of the baptism of Jesus, when the Holy Spirit descended upon Him, marked the fulfillment of Daniel's prophecy that the most holy would be <u>anointed</u>. That day also marked the beginning of the ministry of Jesus, the <u>Messiah Prince,</u> upon the earth.

Jesus was anointed at a point 3 and ½ years before the cross. This time period represents the first half of the 70th week of Daniel. During this 3 and ½ year period, Jesus proclaimed and <u>confirmed</u> the gospel of the Kingdom, the <u>Holy Covenant,</u> in a ministry exclusively to the Jews. Then at the midpoint of the 70th week of Daniel, Jesus shed his blood on the cross as the final once for all sacrifice for sin <u>causing the sacrifice to cease</u> by putting to an end the animal sacrifice for sins according to the law.

After the cross the time period of the church age is not counted in the 70 weeks of Daniel. Currently, there still remains to be fulfilled the second half of the 70th week of Daniel. This will be fulfilled by Messiah in a ministry once again exclusively to the Jews who will be the 144,000 protected in the wilderness during the 3 and ½ year tribulation period.

Daniel's seventy weeks are actually 70 weeks of years, or 70 x 7 years, or 490 years. The important events of the future concerning the people of Israel and the city of Jerusalem will be contained within the 70 weeks of years. As seen in Daniel 9:25 there would be 69 weeks from the command to restore and build Jerusalem unto the Messiah the Prince. 69 X 7 = 483 years.

483 years was the actual time from the command to rebuild Jerusalem until the ministry of Jesus began on earth. The initiation of the ministry of Jesus with the anointing of Jesus the Messiah Prince marked the beginning of the 70th or final week of Daniel. The death of Jesus on the cross caused the sacrifice to cease. This occurred at the midpoint of the 70th week of Daniel.

Daniel 9:24*Seventy weeks are determined upon thy people and upon thy holy city, to finish the transgression, and to make an end of sins, and to make reconciliation for iniquity, and to bring in everlasting righteousness, and to seal up the vision and prophecy, and to anoint the most Holy.* ***25*** *Know therefore and understand, that from the going forth* *of the commandment to restore and to build Jerusalem unto the <u>Messiah the Prince</u> shall be seven weeks, and threescore and two weeks: the street shall be built again, and the wall, even in troublous times.*

Sixty nine weeks, the time until the Messiah the Prince, is divided into two separate periods of seven weeks and sixty two weeks. Why? The purpose of the time being divided into two separate periods is to mark the occurrence of significant events during the overall timeline.

Israel's exile that occured during the days of Daniel ended just as Daniel prophesied. Following Israel's release from captivity in the first <u>seven weeks</u> or 49 years the temple was rebuilt. After the first seven weeks, came the next <u>62 weeks</u> or 434 years. There were 434 years from the point the temple was rebuilt until the arrival on earth of the ministry of Messiah the Prince.

Daniel 9:26 *And after threescore and two weeks shall <u>Messiah</u> be cut off, but not for himself: and the people of <u>the prince</u> that shall come shall destroy the city and the sanctuary; and the end thereof shall be with a flood, and <u>unto the end of the war</u> desolations are determined.*

Messiah is <u>the Prince</u> that Daniel prophesied would come. Messiah is <u>the Prince</u> prophesied to come and then be cut off or killed. This was fulfilled on the cross as Messiah was cut off just as Daniel prophesied.

As a result of Israel's rejection of Messiah, and rejection of the sacrifice of the blood Jesus shed for the remission of sin, Israel was punished. Daniel prophesied that after Messiah's death, that the Messiah Prince would have a people go to destroy the city of Jerusalem and the sanctuary or temple. This occurred just as Daniel prophesied in 70 AD with the Roman destruction of the temple. The destruction of the temple and the city of Jerusalem was also prophesied by Jesus, and the reason for this punishment is also revealed in that prophecy.

Matthew 24:1 *And Jesus went out, and departed from the temple: and his disciples came to him for to shew him the buildings of the temple.*

2 And Jesus said unto them, See ye not all these things? verily I say unto you, There shall not be left here one stone upon another, that shall not be thrown down.

Luke 19:41 *And when he was come near, he beheld the city, and wept over it, 42 Saying, If thou hadst known, even thou, at least in this thy day, the things which belong unto thy peace! but now they are hid from thine eyes. 43 For the days shall come upon thee, that thine enemies shall cast a trench about thee, and compass thee round, and keep thee in on every side, 44 And shall lay thee even with the ground, and thy children within thee; and <u>they shall not leave in thee one stone upon another</u>; <u>because thou knewest not the time of thy visitation</u>.*

The temple was made desolate because the Jewish nation did not recognize the time of their visitation by Messiah and did not receive him.

In the following passage the desolation of the temple is prophesied to continue *"<u>unto the end of the war</u>."* This war is the war is with the <u>kingdom of darkness</u>. In verse 27 below we see that, *"he shall make it desolate, even until the consummation..."* The term *"consummation"* means the end. The temple shall remain desolate, in ruins, to the end because the Jews, overall as a nation, did not recognize the time of their visitation by their Messiah Prince the Lord Jesus Christ.

Daniel 9:26 *And after threescore and two weeks shall <u>Messiah</u> be cut off, but not for himself: and the people of the prince that shall come shall destroy the city and the sanctuary; and the end thereof shall be with a flood, and unto the end of the war desolations are determined. 27 And **he** shall confirm the covenant with many for one week: and in the midst of the week **he** shall cause the sacrifice and the oblation to cease, and for the overspreading of abominations he shall make it desolate, even until the consummation, and that determined shall be poured upon the desolate.*

A pronoun in a text must refer to a prior noun defined in that passage of text. The pronoun "he" in the scripture above refers back to the Messiah. The pronoun "he" cannot refer to antichrist who has not been mentioned prior in the text.

The convenant confirmed for a week of seven years is not a seven year peace treaty made by the antichrist. This erroneous interpretation of Daniel 9:27 has led to the pervasive error in popular theology of a seven year tribulation period. The covenant of Daniel 9:27 is not a peace treaty of the antichrist. The covenant of Daniel 9:27 is the Holy Covenant confirmed by the Messiah Prince, who also caused the sacrifice to cease by shedding his own sacrificial blood on the cross.

Tribulation will not last seven years but rather only 3 & 1/2 years as noted repeatedly in the book of Revelation and as we shall also see in Daniel chapter 12. The time span of the 3 & 1/2 year tribulation will be the fulfillment of the second half of the 70th week of Daniel as Jesus will appear to the 144,000 Jews and minister to them the Holy Covenant in their place of protection in the wilderness. The first half of the 70th week of Daniel took place as Jesus ministered the Holy Covenant, also known as the gospel of the Kingdom, to the Jews for the 3 & 1/2 year period prior to his death on the cross.

The term Holy Covenant is specifically seen three times in Daniel chapter 11 in verses 28-30. The Holy Covenant is a covenant of the Lord and is a covenant of the blood of Jesus Christ. The Holy Covenant is the covenant of Daniel chapter 9. It is not a peace treaty the antichrist makes with Israel.

Review of Daniel 9:27...

Daniel 9:27 *And he shall confirm the covenant with many for one week: and in the midst of the week he shall cause the sacrifice and the oblation to cease,*

But in the midst of the week he, the Messiah Prince, caused the sacrifice to cease by permanently putting an end to animal sacrifice with his own death on the cross. Jesus Christ caused the animal sacrificial system according to the law to cease. The covenant is confirmed through the ministry of Jesus the Messiah Prince. The covenant is confirmed with Messiah's proclamation of the gospel of the Kingdom to Israel for a total of 7 years, 3 & ½ years of ministry before the cross and then 3 & ½ years to the 144,000 Jews during tribulation.

This seventieth week of Daniel consists, first of all, of three and one half years of the ministry of Jesus ending at the cross. Then the second ½ of the 70th week of Daniel will begin almost 2000 years later on the day of the Lord when Jesus appears on the Mount of Olives to rescue the 144,000 Jews who have fled Jerusalem. They shall look upon Him whom they have pierced and weep. They shall then be taken to a place of protection in the wilderness. Jesus shall minister confirmation of the Holy Covenant exclusively with these 144,000 Jews for 3 and ½ years during the tribulation and thus complete the second half of the 70th week of Daniel.

The covenant, which is confirmed by Jesus to Israel, is the holy covenant of the Lord. This covenant is also described in Hebrews 10:16.

Hebrews 10:15-17 *Whereof the Holy Ghost also is a witness to us: for after that he had said before, THIS IS THE <u>COVENANT</u> THAT I WILL MAKE WITH THEM AFTER THOSE DAYS, SAITH THE LORD, I WILL PUT MY LAWS INTO THEIR HEARTS, AND IN THEIR MINDS WILL I WRITE THEM; AND THEIR SINS AND INIQUIITIES WILL I REMEMBER NO MORE.*

Daniel 9:27 *...and in the midst of the week <u>he shall cause the sacrifice</u> and the oblation <u>to cease</u>,*

In the midst of the 70th week of Daniel, after the first 3 ½ years of ministry to the Jews, Jesus the Messiah caused the sacrifice to cease by the sacrifice of his own precious blood on the cross.

A man called the antichrist will NOT cause the sacrifice to cease. The sacrifice has already been caused to cease permanently, being taken away once and for all by the sacrifice of the precious blood of Jesus shed once and for all. Jesus has already taken away the sacrifice permanently. Hebrews chapter 10 explains this fact.

Hebrews 10:8 *...Sacrifice and offering and burnt offerings and offering for sin thou wouldest not, neither hadst pleasure therein; which are offered by the law;* ***9*** *Then said he, Lo, I come to do thy will, O God.* <u>*He taketh away the first,*</u> *that he may establish the second.* ***10*** *By the which will we are sanctified through the offering of the body of Jesus Christ once for all.*

Daniel 9:27 *...and in the midst of the week <u>he</u> shall cause the sacrifice and the oblation to cease, and for the overspreading of abominations <u>he</u> shall make it desolate, even until the consummation, and that determined shall be poured upon the desolate.*

The "overspreading of abomination" in the above passage refers to the widespread rejection of Jesus who came in the flesh, and the rejection of the sin cleansing power of the blood of Jesus shed as the final sacrifice for sin. Daniel prophesied that for this overspreading abomination that <u>he</u> would make the sanctuary, the temple desolate. Jesus in Luke 19:44 also prophesied this destruction of the temple because Jews did not recognize the time of their visitation by Messiah.

Luke 19:44 *And shall lay thee even with the ground, and thy children within thee; and they shall not leave in thee one stone upon another;* <u>*because thou knewest not the time of thy visitation*</u>*.*

The Jews rejection of Jesus as the Messiah who came in the flesh was a manifestation of a spirit of antichrist.

1 John 4:3 *And <u>every spirit</u> that confesseth not that Jesus Christ is come in the flesh is not of God: and this is that <u>spirit of antichrist</u>, whereof ye have heard that <u>it should come</u>; and even now already is in the world.*

Because of this overspreading abomination, which was the widespread rejection of Jesus the Messiah, the holy place was made desolate...no more temple... no more animal sacrifices... nothing... desolate.

Daniel 9:27 *...and for the overspreading of abominations he shall make it desolate, even until the consummation...*

The holy place was made desolate just as Daniel prophesied, and it will remain desolate even unto the end or consummation. Contrary to popular opinion, the temple shall not be rebuilt.

Daniel 9:27*...and that determined shall be poured upon the desolate.*

Just as Daniel prophesied, the desolate, the nation of Israel, entered into their final and most severe exile lasting almost 2000 years. This exile finally ended in 1948 when Israel was reborn as a nation on the earth in preparation for the coming of the DAY OF THE LORD.

Daniel chapter 12 presents a vision of events that shall occur on the day of the Lord as the angel Michael stands for the protection and deliverance of the remnant of the nation of Israel, the 144,000 Jews. It also defines this as the time of resurrection. The events of resurrection which precedes rapture and the 144,000 fleeing into the wilderness under the protection of the Lord are events of the day of the Lord occurring at the beginning of the 3 & ½ year tribulation period.

Daniel 12:1 *And at that time shall Michael stand up, the great prince which standeth for the children of thy people: and there shall be a <u>time of trouble</u>, such as never was since there was a nation even to that same time: and at that time thy people shall be delivered, every one that shall be found written in the book.* ***2*** *And many of them that sleep in the dust of the earth shall awake...*

- Michael is an <u>angel</u>.
- Michael will stand up for the <u>children of Daniel's people</u>.
- The children of Daniel's people are the nation of <u>Israel</u>.
- There shall be a <u>time of trouble</u>, such as never was.
- It will be at a time of trouble or <u>tribulation</u>.
- Daniel's people shall be <u>delivered</u>.
- This will also be the time of <u>resurrection</u> of the dead.
- These events occur on the day of the LORD.
- The angel Michael shall be involved in protection of the 144,000 who are taken to a special place in the wilderness on the day of the Lord.

***Daniel 12:5** Then I Daniel looked, and, behold, there stood other two, the one on this side of the bank of the river, and the other on that side of the bank of the river. **6** And one said to the man clothed in linen, which was upon the waters of the river, <u>How long shall it be to the end</u> of these wonders?*

We must carefully remember the question as we examine the answer. The question to be answered is this… From the time Michael stands up as the protector of Israel on the day of the Lord, how long shall it be to the END of tribulation, this time of trouble?

The answer is clear in verse 7 below. 3 & ½ years is the answer given. 3 & ½ years is the length of the tribulation period and 3 & ½ years is the answer given with use of the phrase, *"for a time, times, and an half…"*

***Daniel 12:7** And I heard the man clothed in linen, which was upon the waters of the river, when he held up his right hand and his left hand unto heaven, and sware by him that liveth for ever that it shall be for a time, times, and an half…*

The phrase "for a time, times, and an half" means 3 & ½ years and is seen also in describing the length of the tribulation period in the book of Revelation.

Revelation 12:14 *And to the woman were given two wings of a great eagle, that she might fly into the wilderness, into her place, where she is nourished <u>for a time, and times, and half a time</u>, from the face of the serpent.*

The above scripture refers to the length of time the 144,000 Jews are protected in the wilderness during the tribulation period. It is the time the remnant of the nation of Israel shall be fed in the wilderness during tribulation. Tribulation shall last 3 & ½ years, not seven years.

Chapter 22 The Vision of the Two Nails

The vision of the two nails is a prophetic message previously presented in newspaper and by radio. I present it now to the reader as an admonition even as Joel wrote…

Joel 2:1-2 *Blow ye the trumpet in Zion, and sound an alarm in my holy mountain: let all the inhabitants of the land tremble: for the day of the Lord cometh, for it is nigh at hand;*

The Vision of the Two Nails…

I don't sleep as much as I used to. The Lord wakes me up and shows me things.

I see two very large nails. These sharp spikes are similar to the nails that pierced our precious Lord. I hold the nails, one in each fist with their points toward the ground. As I raise their sharp points higher, I suddenly thrust downward with all my might and strength. I strike downward into the earth with all my might to cause two important days to stick in the consciousness of those on the earth.

The two nails represent two important DAYS that must stick in your mind. The nail in my right hand represents the great and notable DAY OF THE LORD. (Zephaniah 1:12-18, Acts 2:19-21, Revelation 6:12-17)

On the DAY OF THE LORD…
- The sun will turn black as sackcloth.
- The moon will turn blood red.
- A great earthquake will shake every mountain and island on the face of the earth.
- There will be great fear as many men will walk in fear like blind men and hide themselves in caves and rocks.

On the DAY OF THE LORD when the hour of the Lord's judgment is come, an angel having the everlasting gospel (Revelation 14:6) will shout from the midst of heaven with a loud voice to the every nation, and kindred, and tongue, and people saying, "FEAR GOD, and give glory to him; for the hour of his judgment is come: and worship him that made heaven, and earth, and the sea, and the fountains of waters."

Many will fear God on the DAY OF THE LORD, call on the name of Jesus, and be saved. This will be a sovereign harvest done by the Lord and will fulfill Matthew 24:14 as the angel preaches the everlasting gospel in all the world for a witness unto all nations. Then the end will come.

On the DAY OF THE LORD, whosoever shall call on the name of the Lord shall be saved. His name is Jesus. There is no other name by which men can be saved.

It is the grace of God that will literally shake the earth and send an angel to preach the gospel to all nations on the great DAY OF THE LORD. That day will be a sovereign move of God bringing a great and sudden harvest into His kingdom at the final moment.

Many will remain in fear and unbelief, but many others will be like the thief on the cross crying out at the last moment, "Jesus, Lord remember me when you come in your kingdom." And like the thief on the cross, everyone who calls on the name of Jesus will be with Jesus in paradise on that great and notable DAY OF THE LORD.

On the DAY OF THE LORD the dead in Christ will rise from their graves and begin to rise off the earth. We who are alive, and have called on the name Jesus for salvation, will rise up together in the clouds to meet the Lord in the air and so shall we ever be with the Lord.

Isaiah 55:6 says, *"Seek ye the Lord while he may be found..."*

There is a day coming when men will no longer be able to seek and find the Lord because the DAY OF THE LORD will be the final day of grace on the earth. As it was in the days of Noah, so shall it be on the DAY OF THE LORD. When God closed the door to the ark everyone left behind was destroyed.

All those who are LEFT BEHIND, those who are not God's children, will remain on the earth and will be given over to strong delusion and will worship the beast. They will suffer in the midst of tribulation and plagues and will drink the wine of God's wrath poured out upon the earth. These will all ultimately be killed by the end of the tribulation period. Their eternal home will be the lake of fire.

Of all the nations on earth, only the nation of Israel will be preserved on the earth during the tribulation period. 144,000 of Israel will flee to a special place of protection that God will provide in the wilderness where they shall be nourished for three and one half years.

Zephaniah 1:12-18 tells us that complacent men will say in their heart, *"The Lord will not do good, neither will he do evil."* What will happen to these men? The Lord will bring distress upon them… *"they shall walk like blind men, because they have sinned against the LORD: and their blood shall be poured out as dust, and their flesh as the dung."* ***Zephaniah 1:17***

The DAY OF THE LORD will overtake complacent men like a thief in the night. But we who are saved by grace through faith having our sins washed away by the blood of Jesus are not in darkness that the DAY OF THE LORD should overtake us as a thief.

In my left hand is the other nail. This other nail represents a different day. It is a specific day prophesied to be a sign on the earth indicating that the great DAY OF THE LORD is about to occur.

The prophet Isaiah prophesied this day to be the signal or sign of the impending DAY OF THE LORD. Isaiah called this day THE DAY OF THE GREAT SLAUGHTER…

The prophet Isaiah called this day…THE DAY OF THE GREAT SLAUGHTER WHEN THE TOWERS FALL. I am not making this up. It is in your Bible…Isaiah 30:25-30 KJV The prophet Ezekiel also saw this day, prophesying the fall of the world trade center…

*…THY MERCHANDISE AND ALL THY COMPANY IN THE MIDST OF THEE SHALL FALL. ALL THE INHABITANTS OF THE ISLES SHALL BE ASTONISHED AT THEE, AND THEIR KINGS SHALL BE SORE AFRAID… **Ezekiel 27:34&35***

THE DAY OF THE GREAT SLAUGHTER WHEN THE TOWERS FELL, was the beginning of sorrows and was a sign on the earth indicating that the DAY OF THE LORD is about to occur. Acts 2:19 tells us that the sign on the earth signaling the impending DAY OF THE LORD are the signs of <u>blood, and fire, and vapor of smoke</u>.

When was the day of the great slaughter when the towers fell? What did we see on that day? The <u>entire world</u> saw blood, and fire, and vapor of smoke.

Ask any elementary classroom in this nation what was THE DAY OF THE GREAT SLAUGHTER WHEN THE TOWERS FELL? They will all say 9-11-01. Ask any people or nation on the earth and they will say 9-11-01.

September 11th is known over the entire earth as the day of the great slaughter when the towers fell. Everyone knows that day for all nations were astonished by this terror.

THE DAY OF THE GREAT SLAUGHTER WHEN THE TOWERS FELL…will be followed shortly by…

THE GREAT AND NOTABLE DAY OF THE LORD…

The vision of the two nails will cause these two days to stick in your mind.

Don't be LEFT BEHIND. Fear God and call on the name of Jesus for salvation now while you can. The great and notable DAY OF THE LORD is coming quickly. A great flood of fire and tribulation is coming upon the earth and the door of the ark is already lifting off the ground and is about to close tightly. Outside the door will be weeping and the gnashing of teeth. All those who are left behind will be destroyed.

Seek the Lord today, while he may be found.

Say, "Jesus, Lord remember me when you come in your kingdom. Forgive me of my sins. Wash me in your cleansing blood. Jesus come into my heart. Jesus save me." And keep seeking the Lord with all your heart and keep calling on his name. The Lord comes quickly.

Even so, come, Lord Jesus. The grace of our Lord Jesus Christ be with you all. Amen.

APPENDIX
POWERPOINT NOTES FOR ONLINE VIDEO.

The online video presentation includes many paintings and visual references. This presentation can be viewed online at www.biblemystery.com

Mysteries of Revelation Unveiled
Photo by NASA and the Hubble Heritage Team (STScI/AURA) Hubble Telescope STScI-PRCO4-10
Feb. 8, 2004

- Mysteries of Revelation Unveiled
- Presented by
- Joel 2:1 Ministry Partners
- Rev. Terry Gage M.D.
- www.biblemystery.com
- Ordained by ACTS Ministry Springfield, Missouri September 11, 2005
- Professor of Eschatology ACTS Ministry University appointed 2009
- Clinical Associate Professor Texas Tech University School of Medicine Lubbock, Texas
- Special thank you for the anointed art of Pat Marvenko Smith
- www.revelationillustrated.com
- Other artists are sited in the presentation.

Mysteries of Revelation Unveiled
The Kingdom of Heaven
IS AT HAND
GOOD NEWS
Destruction is coming...

- But...
- The Lord has provided you
- a means of escape...
- **Though faith in Jesus...**
- On the day of the Lord
- ...it shall come to pass,

- that whosoever shall call on the name of the Lord shall be saved. Acts 2:21

Mysteries of Revelation Unveiled
Mystery
- **Strong's Number:** 3466 Origin **musthvrion** from a derivative of muo (to shut the mouth)
- hidden thing, secret, mystery
- generally mysteries, religious secrets, confided only to the initiated and not to ordinary mortals
- a hidden or secret thing, not obvious to the understanding

Key to solving a mystery… Attention to the details…
For assistance in this we can ask our super sleuth Sherlock Holmes.

"Holmes, how can we know for sure that our solution to a mystery is correct?"

"Elementary Watson. Attention to detail is the key. And remember Watson if symbolism is a factor in the mystery, the definition of the symbolism will be detailed and defined in scripture. Otherwise it is not symbolic it is literal."

Example of the mystery of the seven stars

Revelation 1:20 The mystery of the seven stars which thou sawest in my right hand, and the seven golden candlesticks. The seven stars are the angels of the seven churches…

The mystery is defined by the word of Jesus   stars = angels
"I see Holmes. So you mean every time we see the word star we can know that this is symbolic of an angel."
"Precisely Watson."

Mysteries, riddles, puzzles
- Offer a sense of challenge
- Excitement, expectation

- Fulfillment on discovery solution
- These are all enhanced with mysteries of the book of Revelation
- When we see true solution we know that the time is at hand.

Mystery of the beast that was, and is not, and yet is. Revelation 17:8

Three Key Principles
- Only the Spirit of the living God can reveal such mysteries to mankind.
- Solutions come in answer to prayer and with careful attention to details
- Keen focus on the words in RED the words Jesus spoke about the end time

This photograph is a 1000 piece jigsaw puzzle with artwork from Michelangelo's masterpiece painting on the ceiling of the Sistine Chapel. If a few pieces were out of place, where the finger of God touches the finger of Adam, the entire message of this masterpiece would be lost.

Mysteries of Revelation Putting the puzzle pieces together correctly... We have to work and rearrange the pieces, until our puzzle matches the picture on the cover of the box.

The Words of Jesus are the key to putting the puzzle together accurately.
- The picture on the outside of the puzzle box are the words written in red in your Bible...
- The picture Jesus paints of the end time.

In Luke 21 Jesus is speaking of that coming day...

Luke 21:35 For as a snare shall it come on all them that dwell on the face of the whole earth.

This is the photograph of an animal whose destruction came by the slow, painful, and frantic death of a snare.

Luke 21:35 *For as a <u>snare</u> shall it come on <u>all them that dwell</u> on the face of the whole earth.*

A Mystery…
"But Holmes, if that day comes as a snare of destruction on <u>all them that dwell on the face of the whole earth</u>. Who can be saved?"
"Elementary Watson. Evacuation is their only hope. They must not be LEFT BEHIND!"

Luke 21:36 *Watch ye therefore, and pray always, that ye may be accounted worthy to <u>escape</u> all these things that shall come to pass, and <u>to stand before the Son of man</u>.*

- We can be worthy to escape by one thing…
- The blood of Jesus Christ
- Shed for the forgiveness of sins

Escape…
- Strong's definition of the word <u>escape</u>
- To seek safety in flight
- Phrase <u>escape to</u>…
- Tells where you are to go in flight
- Jesus said escape… to stand before the Son of Man
- Where is the Son of man?
- The right hand of the Father at the throne in heaven.

In this painting, these, in the clouds, have escaped in flight to stand before the Son of Man before the throne.

Parable of the Ten VirginsArt by Bo

Matthew 25:1 *Then shall the kingdom of heaven be likened unto ten virgins, which took their lamps, and went forth to meet the bridegroom.*

2 And five of them were wise, and five were foolish. 3 They that were foolish took their lamps, and took no oil with them:4 But the wise took oil in their vessels with their lamps.5 While the bridegroom tarried, they all slumbered and slept. 6 And at midnight there was a cry made, Behold, the bridegroom cometh; go ye out to meet him... 8 And the foolish said unto the wise, Give us of your oil; for our lamps are gone out. 9 But the wise answered, saying, Not so; lest there be not enough for us and you: but go ye rather to them that sell, and buy for yourselves. 10 And while they went to buy, the bridegroom came; and they that were ready went in with him to the marriage: and the <u>door was shut</u>. 11 Afterward came also the other virgins, saying, Lord, Lord, open to us. 12 But he answered and said, Verily I say unto you, I know you not. 13 Watch therefore, for ye know neither the day nor the hour wherein the Son of man cometh.

Painting of the parable of the ten virgins...Peter von Cornelius 1783

Isaiah 55:6 *Seek ye the LORD while he may be found,*

- Isaiah knew that a day was coming when it would be too late to seek and find the Lord.
- Jesus taught this clearly in the parable of the ten virgins

Luke 17:24 *For as the lightning, that lighteneth out of the one part under heaven, shineth unto the other part under heaven; so shall also the Son of man be <u>in his day</u>.*

What is his day? His day is <u>the day of the Lord</u>.

Luke 17:26 *And as it was in the days of Noe, so shall it be...*

While the ark was prepared...

Luke 17:27 *They did eat, they drank, they married wives, they were given in marriage, until the day that Noe entered into the ark, and the flood came, and destroyed them all.*

Luke 17:30 *Even thus shall it be in the day when the Son of man is revealed.*

Luke 17:28 *Likewise also as it was in the days of Lot; they did eat, they drank, they bought, they sold, they planted, they builded;* ***29*** *But the same day that Lot went out of Sodom it rained fire and brimstone from heaven, and destroyed them all.* ***30*** *Even thus shall it be in the day when the Son of man is revealed.* ***31*** *In that day, he which shall be upon the housetop, and his stuff in the house, let him not come down to take it away: and he that is in the field, let him likewise not return back.* <u>Remember Lot's wife.</u>

Luke 17:33 *Whosoever shall seek to save his life shall lose it; and whosoever shall lose his life shall preserve it.*

Luke 17:35 *Two women shall be grinding together; the one shall be taken, and the other left.*

Luke 17:36 *Two men shall be in the field; the one shall be taken, and the other left.*

…<u>one shall be taken, and the other left</u>.

Note above some shall be taken and the others shall be left behind. Do not be left behind…REMEMBER LOT'S WIFE. She looked back longing to remain in her old life and did not escape.

Luke 17:36&37*…one shall be taken, and the other left. And they answered and said unto him, <u>Where, Lord</u>? And he said unto them, Wheresoever the body is,… thither will the eagles be gathered together.*

The disciples asked where these people are being taken to. Jesus answers with a mystery…. *"Wheresoever the body is,… thither will the eagles be gathered together."*

"Holmes, is this the vultures feeding on the dead bodies at Armagedon?"

"Nonsense Watson. The clue is in understanding which body Jesus is referring to."

"Which body is that Holmes?"

"Elementary Watson. The <u>body of Christ,</u> the ark of safety in Christ. The body of Christ shall be taken to a place where eagles gather."

"But Holmes. Where do eagles gather?"

"Elementary Watson. Eagles gather soaring high in the sky. That is where the body of Christ shall be taken."

"Brilliant Holmes…the rapture of the Church!"

"Precisely Watson."

Consider ***Isaiah 40:31*** *But they that wait upon the LORD shall renew their strength; <u>they shall mount up with wings as eagles</u>; they shall run, and not be weary; and they shall walk, and not faint.*

Matthew 24:29 *Immediately <u>after</u> the tribulation of those days shall the sun be darkened, and the moon shall not give her light, and the stars shall fall from heaven, and the powers of the heavens shall be shaken:*

Because we shall see clearly from the old testament prophets that the specific events described in this verse shall indeed occur immediately **<u>with</u>** the onset of the tribulation period, we must look at the Greek word which was translated here as "<u>after</u>."

Strong's definition or "<u>after</u>" Matthew 24 vs 29
- Strong's Number: 3326
- metav primary preposition (often used adverbially)
- with, after, behind
- King James Word Usage - Total: <u>with 345,</u> after 88, among 5,
- So most often metav was translated as **with** in the King James
- If the KJV translators used **with**, the meaning of the passage would clearly look much different and clearly fit the picture of the end times documented by the many scriptures we shall study.

Matthew 24:29 Immediately (__with?__) the tribulation of those days shall the sun be darkened, and the moon shall not give her light...

Matthew 24:30 And then shall appear the sign of the Son of man in heaven: and then shall all the tribes of the earth mourn, and they shall see the Son of man coming in the clouds of heaven with power and great glory.

Painting of Jesus Coming in the Clouds

Matthew 24:31And he shall send his angels with a great sound of a trumpet, and they shall gather together his elect...

We will see that these events do occur immediately with the onset of the tribulation period.

Mystery Why will it not be possible for elect to be deceived?

In **Mark 13:22** Jesus said, "...*false prophets shall rise, and shall shew signs and wonders, to seduce, if it were possible, even the elect.*"

"*false prophets shall rise, and shall shew signs and wonders*"

The false prophet and the beast Apollyon shall rise. They shall rise or ascend out of the bottomless pit. The false prophet shall call down fire from heaven. The awesome power of this sign would deceive even the elect if it were possible. What will happen to make it not possible for the elect to be deceived? We see the solution to this mystery as the passage continues in verse 26.

Mark 13:26 And then shall they see the Son of man coming in the clouds with great power and glory. 27 And then shall he send his angels, and shall gather together his elect...

The elect shall be gathered and taken up by the angels.

It will not be possible for the elect to be deceived for they will be gathered by the angels in the rapture to escape the deception and stand before the Son of man in heaven.

"But Holmes, if the elect who have the Spirit of God must be evacuated to escape deception, what HOPE do the unsaved have who are left behind?"

"Elementary Watson! The answer is NONE. No hope for those LEFT BEHIND."

"But Holmes, what percentage left behind will take the mark?"

"Elementary Watson. ALL. 100% of those left behind will take the mark."

Revelation 13:16 *And he causeth **all**, both small and great, rich and poor, free and bond, to receive a mark...*

"But, but, but..Holmes!"

"All in good time Watson as the mystery unfolds. But most important Watson, keep clear vision of the words in red in your Bible the words of Jesus."

"But HOLMES! What of the martyrs beheaded for refusing the mark?"

"Remember the two witnesses Watson. The scriptures you refer to are all precisely fulfilled by the death of just the two witnesses as we shall see."

Two signs of His Coming

Acts 2:19 *And I will shew wonders in heaven above, and signs in the earth beneath; blood, and fire, and vapour of smoke:*

Mystery. Sign on the earth blood, and fire, and vapour of smoke
The details...Words of the Prophets Isaiah and Ezekiel

Accurately saw events of 9-11-01 as the sign indicating that the day of the Lord is near.

The prophet Isaiah could see key events far into the future...700years before the birth of Jesus Christ, Isaiah wrote...

He was wounded for our transgressions
He was bruised for our iniquities
The chastisement of our peace was upon Him
and with His stripes we are healed. **Isaiah 53:5**

Isaiah 53:6 *All we like sheep have gone astray; we have turned every one to his own way; and the LORD hath laid on him the iniquity of us all.*

Isaiah saw the suffering our Lord Jesus Christ 700 years before the cross. Isaiah looked thousands of years ahead to see the event that would signal the return of Jesus Christ...

He called that event precisely...THE DAY OF THE GREAT SLAUGHTER WHEN THE TOWERS FALL.

THE DAY OF THE GREAT SLAUGHTER WHEN THE TOWERS FALL

Isaiah 30:25 *And there shall be upon every high mountain, and upon every high hill, rivers and streams of waters in the day of the great slaughter, when the towers fall.*

It was a sign on the earth of blood, and fire, and vapour of smoke
Then, Isaiah describes the event that is to occur <u>just after</u> the day of the great slaughter when the towers fall...

Isaiah 30:27 *Behold, the name of <u>the LORD cometh from far,</u> burning with his anger, and the burden thereof is heavy: his lips are full of indignation, and his tongue as a devouring fire: his tongue as a devouring fire...*

"But Holmes was 911 really the sign?"

"Watson. Look at the evidence. Old Testament prophets detail an end time fall of a towering world trade center..."

Tyrus + Babylon are symbolic names of the end time merchant city for many nations...a world trade center whose towers come crashing to the ground just prior to the return of the Lord Jesus Christ.

Isaiah 23:1 The burden of Tyre. Howl, ...for it is laid waste...
2 Be still, ye inhabitants of the isle; thou whom the merchants of Zidon, that pass over the sea, have replenished...

*3...and **she is a mart of nations**.*

Isaiah 23:8 Who hath taken this counsel against Tyre, the <u>crowning city</u>, whose <u>merchants</u> are princes, whose traffickers are the honourable of the earth? 9 The LORD of hosts hath purposed it, to stain the pride of all glory, and to bring into contempt all the honourable of the earth.

THEN A FEW VERSES LATER...

Isaiah 24:1 Behold, the LORD maketh the earth empty, and maketh it waste, and turneth it upside down, and scattereth abroad the inhabitants thereof.

NOTE:
First in the above passage...
- The laying waist of "the **crowning city**," the "mart of nations"
- Then the day of the LORD as "*the LORD maketh the earth empty, and maketh it waste...*"

Another vision...Isaiah 26

Isaiah 26:2 Open ye the gates, that the righteous nation which keepeth the truth may enter in...

5 For he bringeth down them that dwell on high; the lofty city, he layeth it low; he layeth it low, even to the ground; he bringeth it even to the dust.

Then...

Isaiah 26:19 *Thy dead men shall live, together with my dead body shall they arise. Awake and sing, ye that dwell in dust: for thy dew is as the dew of herbs, and the earth shall cast out the dead. 20 Come, my people, enter thou into thy chambers, and shut thy doors about thee: hide thyself as it were for a little moment, until the indignation be overpast. 21 For, behold, the LORD cometh out of his place to punish the inhabitants of the earth for their iniquity: the earth also shall disclose her blood, and shall no more cover her slain.*

What does Isaiah say is the event that precedes tribulation?

- The mart of nations
- The crowning city
- The lofty city,
- he layeth it low; he layeth it low, even to the ground; he bringeth it even to the dust
- Then resurrection
- Then rapture
- Then punishment on those left behind

On 911 Demonic forces were given free reign to destroy...

- Prelim and foretaste of tribulation
- During tribulation
- Demonic forces will be given free reign
- Not just at ground zero
- But over the entire earth

Ezekiel 26:4 *And they shall destroy the walls of Tyrus, and break down her towers: I will also scrape her dust from her, and make her like the top of a rock.*

Ezekiel 26:9 *And he shall set engines of war against thy walls, and with his axes he shall break down thy towers.*

"...engines of war against thy walls, and with his axes he shall break down thy towers."

Ezekiel 27:3 *And say unto Tyrus, <u>O thou that art situate at the entry of the sea</u>, which <u>art a merchant of the people for many isles</u>, Thus saith the Lord GOD; O Tyrus, thou hast said, I am of perfect beauty.*

"...a <u>merchant</u> of the people for many isles."

Ezekiel 27:32 *And in their wailing they shall take up a lamentation for thee, and lament over thee, saying, What city is like Tyrus...?*

Ezekiel 27:33 *...thy wares went forth out of the seas,...thou didst enrich the kings of the earth with the multitude of thy riches and of thy merchandise. 34...<u>thy merchandise and all thy company in the midst of thee shall fall</u>. 35All the inhabitants of the isles shall be astonished at thee, and their kings shall be sore afraid...*

Tyrus and Babylon are symbolic names of the tower city of merchants, (WTC) that falls in the end time.

The towers of the world trade center were a re-enactment of the tower of Babel...i.e. Babylon.

Tower of Babel re-enacted, is the city of Babylon, a merchant city that falls to announce the impending return of the Lord

Babylon = Ibb original language
Strongs Definition Babel or Babylon = "confusion (by mixing)"

Then they said, *"Come, let us build ourselves a city, and a tower with its top in the heavens, and let us <u>make a name</u> for ourselves...* **Genesis 11:4**

Twin Towers
- Built to make a name for the world financial system.
- ? Root of all evil… the love of money.
- World financial system is one of 7 major principalities under rule of the kingdom of darkness. (Satan's favorite)
- Towers represented an idol on the earth

Joel 2:1 Blow ye the trumpet in Zion,
and sound an alarm in my holy mountain:
let all the inhabitants of the land tremble:
for the day of the LORD is coming

What are we to do?
- Preach the gospel
- Sound the alarm
- Sound an accurate clear alarm
- Watch and DECLARE what you see coming.
- What are we watching for…
- The coming four horsemen of the apocalypse
- The coming of Jesus Christ the lion of Juda

Isaiah 21:6 For thus hath the Lord said unto me, Go, set a watchman, let him declare what he seeth. 7 And he saw a chariot with a couple of horsemen… …and he hearkened diligently with much heed: 8 And he cried, A lion: My lord, I stand continually upon the watchtower in the daytime, and I am set in my ward whole nights: 9 And, behold, here cometh a chariot of men, with a couple of horsemen. (note: two more makes four.) *And he answered and said, Babylon is fallen, is fallen; and all the graven images of her gods he hath broken unto the ground.* (note: the sign that they are coming)

Babylon is fallen, is fallen.
- First tower 1
- Then tower 2
- Thus is the solution to the mystery of Revelation chapter 18
- A towering city of the worlds merchants and traders

- Thrown down with violence ...
- *"like a great millstone... cast into the sea..." Revelation 18:21*
- Prophesied by Isaiah... *"Babylon is fallen, is fallen..."* **Isaiah 21:9**

Key clue to all the mysteries...
- The angelic beasts
- We shall study them in detail

Key to the mysteries of Revelation

Revelation 4:6 *And before the throne there was a sea of glass like unto crystal:and in the midst of the throne, and round about the throne, were four beasts full of eyes before and behind. 7 And the first beast was like a lion, and the second beast like a calf, and the third beast had a face as a man, and the fourth beast was like a flying eagle.*

Revelation 4:8
And the four beasts had each of them <u>*six wings*</u> *about him; and they were full of eyes within: and they rest not day and night, saying,* <u>*Holy, holy, holy,*</u> *Lord God Almighty, which was, and is, and is to come.*

Isaiah also saw what John saw...

Isaiah 6:1 *In the year that king Uzziah died I saw also the Lord sitting upon a throne, high and lifted up, and his train filled the temple. 2 Above it stood the seraphims: each one had* <u>*six wings*</u>*; with twain he covered his face, and with twain he covered his feet, and with twain he did fly. 3 And one cried unto another, and said,* <u>*Holy, holy, holy,*</u> *is the LORD of hosts: the whole earth is full of his glory. 4 And the posts of the door moved at the voice of him that cried, and the house was filled with smoke.*

- The angelic beasts are angels of great power.
- Their voices can shake the door posts in the temple of God in heaven.

"Write that down Watson. The angelic beasts are angels of tremendous power and authority."

"AMAZING HOLMES!"

Two signs of His Coming

Acts 2:19 And I will shew <u>wonders in heaven</u> above, and signs in the earth beneath; blood, and fire, and vapour of smoke:

Wonders in Heaven Feb. 8, 2004
Hubble Space Telescope Photograph

"Holmes, NASA states the central light in this dramatic photograph is 600,000 times more brilliant than our sun. Amazing!"

"Write that number down Watson."

"Is it symbolic?"

"We shall see, Watson, we shall see."

Ezekiel's vision
Ezekiel 1:4-5 And I looked, and, behold, a whirlwind came out of the north, a great cloud, and a fire infolding itself, ...and a brightness was about it,... ...and out of the midst thereof as the colour of amber, out of the midst of the fire...... Also out of the midst thereof came the likeness of four living creatures...

The 4 angelic beasts
Ezekiel 1:10
- *As for the likeness of their faces, they four had the face of a man,*
- *and the face of a lion, on the right side:*
- *and they four had the face of an ox on the left side;*
- *they four also had the face of an eagle.*

The 4 angelic beasts
Ezekiel 1:11
- *Thus were their faces:*
- *and their wings were stretched upward;*

- *two wings of every one were joined one to another,*
- *and two covered their bodies…*
- *…and their appearance and their work*
- *was as it were a wheel in the middle of a wheel.*

Are you able to see characteristics of the angelic beasts in the photograph? Perhaps you need Sherlock Holmes to help you. See the dramatic Hubble Space Telescope Photograph showing characteristics of the four angelic beasts and the space video photography of the wheel in the middle of a wheel at www.biblemystery.com

GOOD NEWS THE COMING REVIVAL OF GRACE PREACHED BY AN ANGEL THE KINGDOM OF HEAVEN REVIVAL

1 Thessalonians 4:16 *For the Lord himself shall descend from heaven with a shout, with the voice of the archangel, and with the trump of God…*

Mystery…What will the voice of the Arch Angel be proclaiming?
Jesus prophesied the Kingdom of Heaven Revival to be preached supernaturally.

Matthew 24:14 And this gospel of the kingdom shall be preached in all the world for a witness unto all nations; and then shall the end come.

John saw the vision.
Revelation 14:6 And I saw another angel fly in the midst of heaven, having the everlasting gospel to preach unto them that dwell on the earth, and to every nation, and kindred, and tongue, and people…
7 Saying with a loud voice,
Fear God, and give glory to him; for the hour of his judgment is come: and worship him that made heaven, and earth, and the sea, and the fountains of waters.

On The Day of the Lord

***Acts 2:20** The sun shall be turned into darkness, and the moon into blood, before* (before the face of) *that great and notable day of the Lord come:* ***21** And it shall come to pass, that whosoever shall call on the name of the Lord shall be saved.*

When the day of the Lord comes the angel shall preach the everlasting gospel across the earth. All the inhabitants of the earth shall hear the gospel in that hour. A great multitude shall call on the name of the Lord Jesus and be saved.

... it shall come to pass, that <u>whosoever shall call on the name of the Lord shall be saved</u>. ***Acts 2:21***

- A final call of grace... THE KINGDOM OF HEAVEN REVIVAL
- Preached by an angel
- To every ear on earth
- On the day of the Lord
- When the hour of His judgment has come

Events of the day of the Lord

***Mark 13:24**...the <u>sun shall be darkened, and the moon shall not give her light</u>, And the stars of heaven shall fall, and the powers that are in heaven shall be shaken.*

As the earth is shaking and the sun goes dark, as every eye sees Jesus coming on the clouds in power and glory a great angel shall shout, "FEAR GOD!" And this angel shall preach the everlasting gospel to every ear on earth. The rapture of the Church shall occur.

***Mark 13:26-27** And then shall they see the Son of man coming in the clouds with great power and glory. And then shall he send his angels, and shall <u>gather</u> together <u>his elect</u>...*

Events of day of the Lord
- Sun dark, moon blood
- Whole earth shaking earthquake
- Stars falling
- Heaven rolled back like a scroll
- Every eye sees Jesus
- Angel declaring "FEAR GOD" and preaching the final gospel message
- Rapture of the Church

Many will fear God and call on the name of the Lord.
- Many others, like Lot's wife will cling to this life on earth rather than going up to meet the Lord in the clouds.
- They will hide in caves and rocks.
- They will cling to this life on earth and be left behind
- What will those LEFT BEHIND face on the day of the LORD?

Isaiah 13:9-10 **The day of the LORD**

Behold, the day of the LORD cometh, cruel both with wrath and fierce anger, to lay the land desolate: and he shall destroy the sinners thereof out of it. For the stars of heaven and the constellations thereof shall not give their light: the sun shall be darkened in his going forth, and the moon shall not cause her light to shine.

Isaiah 13:11 And I will punish the world for their evil, and the wicked for their iniquity; and I will cause the arrogancy of the proud to cease, and will lay low the haughtiness of the terrible.

Zephaniah chapter 1 The Day of the Lord

Zephaniah 1:14 The great day of the LORD is near, it is near, and hasteth greatly, even the voice of the day of the LORD: the mighty man shall cry there bitterly. 17 And I will bring distress upon men, that they shall walk like blind men, because they have sinned against the LORD: and their blood shall be poured out as dust, and their flesh as the dung. 18 Neither their silver nor their gold shall be able to deliver them in the *day of the LORD'S wrath; but the whole land shall be devoured by the fire of his jealousy for he shall make even a <u>speedy riddance of all</u> them that dwell in the land.*

Isaiah 2:12 For **the day of the LORD** *of hosts shall be upon every one that is proud and lofty, and upon every one that is lifted up; and he shall be brought low...**19** And they shall go into the holes of the rocks, and into the caves of the earth, for fear of the LORD, and for the glory of his majesty, when he ariseth to shake terribly the earth....**21** To go into the clefts of the rocks, and into the tops of the ragged rocks, for fear of the LORD, and for the glory of his majesty, when he ariseth to shake terribly the earth.*

*...<u>the day of the Lord</u> so cometh as a thief in the night. **1Thes.5:2***

- *For the Lord himself shall descend from heaven with a shout,*
- *with the voice of the archangel,*
- *and with the trump of God:*
- *and the dead in Christ shall rise first:***1Thes. 4:16**
- *Then **<u>we</u>** which are alive and remain shall be caught up together with them in the clouds, to meet the Lord in the air:***1Thes. 4:17**

<u>We</u> are caught up in air.

- *1 **Thes. 5:2**... the day of the Lord so cometh as a thief in the night.*
- *3 For when **<u>they</u>** shall say, Peace and safety; then sudden destruction cometh upon them, as travail upon a woman with child; and **<u>they shall not escape</u>**.*

We are caught up. They are left behind.
<u>We</u> escape...<u>They</u> do not escape.

*Then **<u>we</u>** which are alive and remain shall be caught up together with them in the clouds, to meet the Lord in the air:* **1Thes. 4:17**

Mystery of the beast that was, and is not, and yet is.
- *The beast that thou sawest <u>was, and is not</u>;*
- *and shall ascend out of the bottomless pit, and go into perdition:*
- *and they that dwell on the earth shall wonder,*
- *whose names were not written in the book of life from the foundation of the world,*
- *when they behold the beast that was, and is not, and yet is.*
Revelation 17:8

Where is the beast? In the bottomless pit.
About the death of the two witnesses at the end of 1260 days of tribulation...

Revelation 11:7 *And when they shall have finished their testimony, the beast that ascendeth out of the bottomless pit shall make war against them, and shall overcome them, and kill them.*

And what is the purpose of this bottomless pit?

Revelation 20:1 *And I saw an angel come down from heaven, having the key of the bottomless pit and a great chain in his hand. 2 And he laid hold on the dragon, that old serpent, which is the Devil, and Satan, and bound him a thousand years, 3 And cast him into the bottomless pit...*

Note: The pit is a prison for fallen angels. But what type of angel is a beast?

Revelation 4:6 *And before the throne there was a sea of glass like unto crystal: and in the midst of the throne, and round about the throne, were four <u>beasts</u>...*

"But Holmes. Why would an angelic beast be locked in the pit in the first place?"
"Elementary Watson. Rebellion!"

"Holmes, do you mean that there were once other angelic beasts around the throne who fell in rebellion?"

"Precisely Watson!"
- We know that 1/3 of all angels fell in the rebellion.
- Which means there must have been 6 angelic beasts before the rebellion.
- Four remain around the throne
- And two fell.
- These two are locked up in the bottomless pit today.
- One of the fallen angelic beasts is the ring leader.
- And the other is his sidekick.
- Which explains the mystery of the two beasts described in Revelation ch. 13

"Holmes, Rebellion of the angelic beasts!"
"Precisely Watson. And the solution to our mystery..."
- The beast *was*...
- at the throne,
- and now *is not,*
- The beast *shall ascend out of the bottomless pit,*
- *and go into perdition.*

Revelation 17:8 *...and they that dwell on the earth shall wonder, whose names were not written in the book of life from the foundation of the world, when they behold the beast that was, and is not, and yet is.*

And when does the beast come out of the pit? It could only be when the pit is opened!

Revelation 9:11 *And they had a king over them, which is the angel of the bottomless pit, whose name in the Hebrew tongue is Abaddon, but in the Greek tongue hath his name Apollyon.*

The beast is the angel of the bottomless pit... Apollyon the destroyer

Revelation 17:8 *...and <u>they that dwell on the earth shall wonder</u>, whose names were not written in the book of life from the foundation of the world, <u>when they behold the beast</u> that was, and is not, and yet is.*

The Mystery of 911

In the first book in the Bible... Genesis <u>9:11</u> Tells of the first destruction of the world by a flood...

In the last book in the Bible...Revelation <u>9:11</u> Tells of the coming destruction with the release from the bottomless pit of Apollyon the Destroyer.

And a day we know as 911 – was Isaiah's sign of coming destruction... The day of the great slaughter when the towers fall.

But we have Good News in the middle book of the Bible... Psalms <u>91:1</u> Tells of our preservation on the day of the Lord. *He who dwells in the secret place... A thousand may fall at your side... ...but it shall not come near you for... ...He shall send his angels... and they shall BEAR YOU UP...!*

Psalms 91 prophesies the rapture of the Church on the day of the Lord.

- Who is the man of lawlessness?
- AKA the beast
- AKA the antichrist.

The first question we must ask is if this man of lawlessness is a descendant of ADAM?

"Holmes, what else could he be?"

"Elementary Watson. Consider..."

Daniel 9:21 *Yea, whiles I was speaking in prayer, even **the man** Gabriel, whom I had seen in the vision at the beginning, being caused to fly swiftly, touched me about the time of the evening oblation.*

Is the man Gabriel a descendant of ADAM? Consider also…

Isaiah 14:12 *How art thou fallen from heaven, O Lucifer, son of the morning! how art thou cut down to the ground, which didst weaken the nations!* **13** *For thou hast said in thine heart, I will ascend into heaven, I will exalt* **my throne** *above the stars of God: I will sit also upon the mount of the congregation, in the sides of the north: (note: the original rebellion…)* **15** *Yet thou shalt be brought down to hell, to the sides of the pit.* **16** *They that see thee shall narrowly look upon thee, and consider thee, saying, Is this the* **man** *that made the earth to tremble,*

"Watson! The fallen angel Lucifer is referred to as <u>a man</u>, but he is an angel."

"Amazing Holmes! That's the answer! The beast, the antichrist, the man of lawlessness is a fallen angel!"

"Precisely Watson. The man of lawlessness is the angel of the bottomless pit… APOLLYON THE DESTROYER."

- Man of lawlessness…the beast
- The angel of the bottomless pit
- Apollyon (destroyer)
- A fallen angelic beast

Man of lawlessness *2 Thes. 2:3* KJV *Let no man deceive you by any means: for that day (the day of the Lord) shall not come…*

- …<u>*unless the apostasy (forsaking) comes first*</u> (Note: The body of Christ shall forsake this earth in the rapture.) **vs. 3** *NASB*
- <u>*and the man of lawlessness is revealed,*</u>
- *the son of <u>destruction</u>.* The Greek word for <u>*destruction*</u> Strong's Number: 684 <u>apoleia</u>
- The man of lawlessness is <u>Apollyon</u>
- A fallen angelic beast <u>Apollyon is the man of lawlessness</u>…

2 Thessalonians 2:4 *NASB who opposes and exalts himself above every so-called god or object of worship, so that <u>he takes his seat in the temple of God</u>, displaying himself as being God.*

NOTE: This is not a future event. It occurred long ago at the initial rebellion in heaven. In the Rebellion… Apollyon and Lucifer attempted to take the throne in the temple of God in heaven.

2 Thessalonians 2:6 *NASB And you know what restrains him now, so that in his time he will be revealed. **7** For the mystery of lawlessness is already at work; only he who now restrains will do so until he is take out of the way. **8** Then that lawless one will be revealed...*

2 Thessalonians 2:9 *KJV Even him, whose coming is after the working of Satan with all power and signs and lying wonders, **10** And with all deceivableness of unrighteousness in them that perish; because they received not the love of the truth, that they might be saved. **11** And for this cause God shall send them strong delusion, that they should believe a lie: **12** That they **<u>all</u>** might be damned who believed not the truth, but had pleasure in unrighteousness.*

The Mystery of the Rapture

Revelation 1:7 *Behold, he cometh with clouds; and every eye shall see him, and they also which pierced him: and all kindreds of the earth shall wail because of him. Even so, Amen.*
Revelation 6:15 *And the kings of the earth, and the great men, and the rich men, and the chief captains, and the mighty men, and every bondman, and every free man, <u>hid themselves in the dens and in the rocks</u> of the mountains; **16** And said to the mountains and rocks, Fall on us, and hide us from the face of him that sitteth on the throne, and from the wrath of the Lamb: **17** For the <u>great day of his wrath</u> is come; and who shall be able to stand?*

"Holmes, popular novels and movies tell of a silent rapture and the mystery of those left behind wondering why so many on earth have suddenly disappeared."

"Nonsense Watson. Every eye shall see the Lord coming on the clouds when he sends his angels to gather the elect. Those left behind shall hide in caves and rocks. They will all know that the day of the Lord's wrath has come. But before we study these events we must look at the mysteries of the seven seals."

Mysteries of the Seven Seals

Revelation 5:1 *And I saw in the right hand of him that sat on the throne a book written within and on the backside, sealed with seven seals.* ***2*** *And I saw a strong angel proclaiming with a loud voice, Who is worthy to open the book, and to loose the seals thereof?* ***3*** *And no man in heaven, nor in earth, neither under the earth, was able to open the book, neither to look thereon.* ***4*** *And I wept much, because no man was found worthy to open and to read the book, neither to look thereon.* ***5*** *And one of the elders saith unto me, Weep not... behold, the Lion of the tribe of Juda, the Root of David, hath prevailed to open the book, and to loose the seven seals thereof.*

A great MYSTERY ...
"Holmes, what does the scroll contain?"

"Elementary Watson. The scroll contains the pronouncements of tribulation punishment to be poured out upon those that dwell on the earth. A key clue Watson. Write this down. A scroll cannot be opened until all of the seven seals are removed. Then and only then... shall the judgments pronounced in the scroll go forth."

Revelation 5:6 *And I beheld, and, lo, in the midst of the throne and of the four beasts, and in the midst of the elders, stood a Lamb as it had been slain, having <u>seven horns</u> and seven eyes, which <u>are the seven Spirits</u> of God sent forth into all the earth.*

"Write this down Watson. Whenever we see <u>horns</u> in the book of Revelation we shall know that horns symbolize <u>spirits</u>."

Revelation 5:9 *And they sung a new song, saying, Thou art worthy to take the book, and to open the seals thereof: for thou wast slain, and hast redeemed us to God by thy blood out of every kindred, and tongue, and people, and nation;*

Revelation 5:14 *And the four beasts said, Amen. And the four and twenty elders fell down and worshipped him that liveth for ever and ever.*

Before we begin to look at the opening of the seven seals we need to skip forward to chapter 7 for an important key clue to the mystery.

- The clue to the mystery of the seals in chapter 6
- Is the strict instruction given to the four angels in chapter 7
- The key is…
- Who are these four angels?

Revelation 7:2 *And I saw another angel ascending from the east, having the seal of the living God: and he cried with a loud voice to the* <u>***four angels***</u>*, to whom it was given to hurt the earth and the sea,…*
3 Saying, <u>*Hurt not the earth,*</u> *neither the sea, nor the trees,* <u>*till we have sealed the servants of our God in their foreheads.*</u>

- The four angels given to hurt the earth
- … are instructed to yet wait…
- They are fallen angels who are not yet permitted to begin their ride of destruction.
- They are the four horsemen of the apocalypse commissioned with the first four seals.

Revelation 6:1*And I saw when the Lamb opened one of the seals, and I heard, as it were the noise of thunder, one of the four beasts saying, Come and see.*

Revelation 6:2 *And I saw, and behold a white horse: and he that sat on him had a bow; and a crown was given unto him: and he went forth conquering, and to conquer.*

Revelation 6:3 *And when he had opened the second seal, I heard the second beast say, Come and see. **4** And there went out another horse that was red: and power was given to him that sat thereon to take peace from the earth, and that they should kill one another: and there was given unto him a great sword.*

Revelation 6:5 *And when he had opened the third seal, I heard the third beast say, Come and see. And I beheld, and lo a black horse; and he that sat on him had a pair of balances in his hand. **6** And I heard a voice in the midst of the four beasts say, A measure of wheat for a penny, and three measures of barley for a penny; and see thou hurt not the oil and the wine.*

Revelation 6:7 *And when he had opened the fourth seal, I heard the voice of the fourth beast say, Come and see. **8** And I looked, and behold a pale horse: and his name that sat on him was **Death,** and Hell followed with him. And power was given unto them over the fourth part of the earth, to kill with sword, and with hunger, and with death, and with the beasts of the earth.*

- We know that the four horsemen are fallen angels because…
- There is an angel named death who is the last enemy to be destroyed. 1 Cor 15:26
- The fallen angels named death and hell will be ultimately be cast into the lake of fire. Revelation 20:14

The four horsemen shall not begin their destructive journey until after the events of chapter 7 where God provides for the preservation of his people.

The first four seals commission four fallen angels to later begin a mission to hurt the earth in the punishment of tribulation. After the forth seal, the fifth seal will be opened. With the opening of the fifth seal we learn that the punishment of tribulation is again withheld and not yet to be released upon the earth.

Revelation 6:9 *And when he had opened the fifth seal, I saw under the altar the souls of them that were slain for the word of God, And they cried with a loud voice, saying,* <u>How long</u>*, O Lord, holy and true, dost thou not judge and* <u>avenge our blood on them that dwell on the earth</u>*?*

Revelation 6:11 *And white robes were given unto every one of them; and it was said unto them, that they should* <u>rest yet for a little season</u>*, ...*
...<u>until their fellowservants also and their brethren, that should be killed as they were, should be fulfilled</u>.

- Only when all the martyrs who shall ever be slain have been slain and are under this altar
- Only then shall the avenging of their blood go forth upon those who remain dwelling upon the earth.
- Only after the last martyr has been slain shall the punishment of tribulation, the avenging of the blood, begin.
- The one exception being the two witnesses.
- Thus
- When we see the avenging of the blood pouring out upon the earth
- we shall know that there shall be no further martyrs killed
- with the exception of the two witnesses.

The events of the day of the Lord begin to take place on the earth with the opening of the sixth seal. Men who refuse Christ shall be <u>hiding in caves and rocks</u>. We also remember that a great angel shall be preaching the gospel in this final hour of grace and those who call on the name of the Lord shall be saved. After the rapture takes place as described in Revelation chapter seven, the seventh seal shall then be opened with the release of tribulation punishment which takes place later on that same great and notable day of the Lord.

Revelation 6:12 *And I beheld when he had opened the sixth seal, and, lo, there was a great earthquake; and the sun became black as sackcloth of hair, and the moon became as blood;*

Revelation 6:15 *And the kings of the earth, and the great men, and the rich men, and the chief captains, and the mighty men, and every bondman, and every free man, <u>hid themselves in the dens and in the rocks</u> of the mountains;* ***16*** *And said to the mountains and rocks, Fall on us, and hide us from the face of him that sitteth on the throne, and from the wrath of the Lamb:*

Revelation 6:17 *For the <u>great day of his wrath</u> is come; and who shall be able to stand?*

The great day of his wrath is the great and notable day of the Lord seen in Acts 2.

The events of chapter seven take place on the day of the Lord. The first event is the sealing of the 144,000 of the children of Israel with the seal of the preservation of God. The second event is the rapture of the church in which is a great multitude taken out of tribulation which is being initiated on earth. These who escape in the rapture are seen standing before the son of Man at the throne in heaven. These events provide for the preservation of God's people prior to the release of tribulation punishment, the avenging of the blood. This punishment shall be poured forth later on the day of the Lord when the seventh seal shall then be opened.

Revelation 7:2 *And I saw another angel ascending from the east, having the seal of the living God: and he cried with a loud voice to the four angels, to whom it was given to hurt the earth and the sea,* ***3*** *Saying,*

Hurt not the earth, neither the sea, nor the trees, till we have sealed the servants of our God in their foreheads.

4 And I heard the number of them which were sealed: and there were sealed an hundred and forty and four thousand of all the tribes of the children of Israel.

144,000 of the children of Israel are taken to a place of protection in the wilderness on earth. The protection of the seal of God is placed in their foreheads. They have escaped the mark of the beast.

Revelation 7:9 *After this I beheld, and, lo, a great multitude, which no man could number, of all nations, and kindreds, and people, and tongues, stood before the throne, and before the Lamb, clothed with white robes...*

Revelation 7:14 *...These are they which came out of great tribulation, and have washed their robes, and made them white in the blood of the Lamb.*

This is the rapture of the church that is taken out of tribulation which is beginning on the earth. These are they who have escaped to stand before the Son of Man just as Jesus said in Luke 21:36. They have escaped the mark of the beast.

"What then Holmes?"
"Elementary Watson. The avenging of the blood."

Revelation 8:1 *And when he had opened the seventh seal, there was silence in heaven about the space of half an hour. And I saw the seven angels which stood before God; and to them were given seven trumpets.*

Revelation 8:3 *And another angel came and stood at the altar, having a golden censer;...and there was given unto him much incense,* that he should offer it with the <u>prayers of all saints</u> upon the golden altar which was before the throne.

"Holmes. What are these prayers of the saints calling for?"
"Elementary Watson. The avenging of their <u>blood</u>."

Revelation 8:5 *And the angel took the censer, and filled it with fire of the altar, and cast it into the earth: and there were voices, and thunderings, and lightnings, and an earthquake. **6** And the seven angels which had the seven trumpets prepared themselves to sound.*

Revelation 8:7 *The first angel sounded, and there followed hail and fire **mingled with blood**, and they were cast upon the earth: and the third part of trees was burnt up, and all green grass was burnt up.*

- The hail and fire are mingled with blood
- because it is the avenging of the <u>blood</u> which is now being poured out.
- The punishment of tribulation has begun.

Revelation 8:8 *And the second angel sounded, and as it were a great mountain burning with fire was cast into the sea: and the third part of the sea became **blood**;*

- With each successive trumpet
- the punishments of tribulation are poured upon those left behind dwelling on the earth.

Revelation 9:1 *And the fifth angel sounded, and I saw a star fall from heaven unto the earth: and to him was given the key of the bottomless pit. **2** And he opened the bottomless pit; and there arose a smoke out of the pit, as the smoke of a great furnace; and the sun and the air were darkened by reason of the smoke of the pit. **3** And there came out of the smoke locusts upon the earth: and unto them was given power, as the scorpions of the earth have power. And it was commanded them* *that they should not hurt the grass of the earth, neither any green thing, neither any tree; but only those men which have not the seal of God in their foreheads. 5 And to them it was given that they should not kill them, but that they should be tormented five months: and their torment was as the torment of a scorpion, when he striketh a man. 6 And in those days shall men seek death, and shall not find it; and shall desire to die, and death shall flee from them.*

Revelation 9:11 *And they had a king over them, which is the angel of the bottomless pit, whose name in the Hebrew tongue is Abaddon, but in the Greek tongue hath his name Apollyon.*

For the first five months of tribulation men shall seek death but shall be unable to find it. For the first five months of tribulation no one shall die. They must suffer the punishment. They shall suffer unbearable torture and domination by the beast Apollyon the destroyer and his army of demonic scorpion locusts.

Then, five months later...

Revelation 9:14 *Saying to the sixth angel which had the trumpet, Loose the four angels which are bound in the great river Euphrates. 15 And the four angels were loosed, which were prepared for an hour, and a day, and a month, and a year, for to slay the third part of men.*
Revelation 9:18 *By these three was the third part of men killed, by the fire, and by the smoke, and by the brimstone, which issued out of their mouths.*
Revelation 9:20 *And the rest of the men which were not killed by these plagues <u>yet repented not</u> ...*
Revelation 9:21 *<u>Neither repented they</u> of their murders, nor of their sorceries, nor of their fornication, nor of their thefts.*

- All those left behind are under strong delusion

- They remain <u>unrepentant</u> to the end, no matter the severity of the plagues

Revelation 11:3 *And I will give power unto my two witnesses, and they shall prophesy a thousand two hundred and threescore days, clothed in sackcloth.*

Revelation 11:5 *And if any man will hurt them, fire proceedeth out of their mouth, and devoureth their enemies: and if any man will hurt them, he must in this manner be killed.* **6** *These have power to shut heaven, that it rain not in the days of their prophecy: and have power over waters to turn them to blood, and to smite the earth with all plagues, as often as they will.* **7** *And when they shall have finished their testimony, the beast that ascendeth out of the bottomless pit shall make war against them, and shall overcome them, and kill them.*

Revelation 11:9 *And they of the people and kindreds and tongues and nations shall see their dead bodies three days and an half, and shall not suffer their dead bodies to be put in graves.* **10***And they that dwell upon the earth shall rejoice over them, and make merry, and shall send gifts one to another; because these two prophets tormented them that dwelt on the earth.* **11** *And after three days and an half the Spirit of life from God entered into them, and they stood upon their feet; and great fear fell upon them which saw them. And they heard a great voice from heaven saying unto them, Come up hither…**12** And they ascended up to heaven in a cloud; and their enemies beheld them.*

Revelation 11:15 *And the seventh angel sounded; and there were great voices in heaven, saying, The kingdoms of this world are become the kingdoms of our Lord, and of his Christ; and he shall reign for ever and ever.*

Revelation 11:19 *And the <u>temple of God was opened in heaven</u>, and there was seen in his temple the ark of his testament: and there were* *lightnings, and voices, and thunderings, and an earthquake, and great hail.*

- The book of Revelation contains a number of visions, some of which describe the same event.
- All of the chapters in the book are not in chronological order.
- We pick up on this same vision of the temple of God in heaven being opened in a later chapter…

Revelation 15:1 *And I saw another sign in heaven, great and marvellous, seven angels having the seven last plagues; for in them is filled up the wrath of God…*
5 And after that I looked, and, behold, the temple of the tabernacle of the testimony in heaven was opened: 6 And the seven angels came out of the temple, having the seven plagues, clothed in pure and white linen, and having their breasts girded with golden girdles. 7 And one of the four beasts gave unto the seven angels seven golden vials full of the wrath of God, who liveth for ever and ever.

Revelation 16:1 *And I heard a great voice out of the temple saying to the seven angels, Go your ways, and pour out the vials of the wrath of God upon the earth. 2 And the first went, and poured out his vial upon the earth; and there fell a noisome and grievous sore upon the men which had the mark of the beast, and upon them which worshipped his image. 3 And the second angel poured out his vial upon the sea; and it became as the blood of a dead man: and every living soul died in the sea.*

With each successive vial the wrath of God is poured out upon those dwelling upon the earth.

Revelation 16:10 *And the fifth angel poured out his vial upon the seat of the beast; and his kingdom was full of darkness; and they gnawed their tongues for pain,*
*11 And blasphemed the God of heaven because of their pains and their sores, and **repented not** of their deeds.*

Revelation 16:17 *And the seventh angel poured out his vial into the air; and there came a great voice out of the temple of heaven, from the throne, saying, It is done.* ***18*** *And there were voices, and thunders, and lightnings; and there was a great earthquake, such as was not since men were upon the earth, so mighty an earthquake, and so great.* ***19*** *And the great city was divided into three parts, and the cities of the nations fell: and great Babylon came in remembrance before God,...*

Revelation 16:21 *And there fell upon men a great hail out of heaven, every stone about the weight of a talent: and men blasphemed God because of the plague of the hail...*

Revelation 19:11 *And I saw heaven opened, and behold a white horse; and he that sat upon him was called Faithful and True, and in righteousness he doth judge and make war....* ***16*** *And he hath on his vesture and on his thigh a name written, KING OF KINGS, AND LORD OF LORDS...* ***19*** *And I saw the beast, and the kings of the earth, and their armies, gathered together to make war against him that sat on the horse, and against his army.* ***20*** *And the beast was taken, and with him the false prophet that wrought miracles before him, with which he deceived them that had received the mark of the beast, and them that worshipped his image... ...These both were cast alive into a lake of fire burning with brimstone.* ***21*** *And the remnant were slain with the sword of him that sat upon the horse, which sword proceeded out of his mouth: and all the fowls were filled with their flesh.*

Advanced Teaching - The Mark of the Beast

Revelation 13:16 *And he causeth all, both small and great, rich and poor, free and bond, to receive a mark in their right hand, or in their foreheads:*

Later we see where the mark of the Lord will be given to the servants of the Lord in heaven.

Revelation 22:3 *And there shall be no more curse: but the throne of God and of the Lamb shall be in it; and his servants shall serve him:* ***4*** *And they shall see his face; and* <u>*his name shall be in their foreheads*</u>*.*

- The mark is a name designating ownership.
- The mark of the Lord in the forehead of his servants will be...
- the name of the Lord.
- In the same way the mark of the beast will be...
- the name of the beast marked in the foreheads of those who are marked for destruction.

What is the mark?
- And that no man might buy or sell, save he that had the mark, or the name of the beast, or the number of his name. Rev.13:17
- The mark is the name of the beast...
- Or the number of his name.
- The number of his name is a number that means symbolically what his name means.
- Here is wisdom. Let him that hath understanding count the number of the beast: for it is the number of a man; and his number is Six hundred threescore and six. Rev. 13:18

Symbolic meaning of numbers
- Certain numbers are considered to have symbolic significance.
- 8 is the number of new beginnings because there were 8 souls saved on the ark during the flood.
- 6 is the number of man symbolically because God created man on the sixth day.
- But 6 is also symbolic of something else in scripture and this meaning matches the meaning of the name of the beast.

Symbolic meaning of 6 and 600 and 666
- Pharaoh sent <u>600</u> chosen chariots to be the destruction of Israel. Exodus 14:7
- The first destruction the flood came in the <u>600</u>th year of Noah's life. Genesis 7:6 & 11

- The name of the beast Apollyon is greek for <u>destruction</u>. The number of his name which is 6 also means <u>destruction</u>.
- 6 and <u>600</u> are both symbolic of destruction
- And 666 is even more emphatic like !!!
- 666 = Destruction-Destruction-Destruction

"But Holmes, what of the mark of the beast… the tiny computer chip?"

"NONSENESE! Watson! The mark is more like a brand for branding cattle, designating ownership. It will be the name of the beast. His name is Apollyon which means destruction. Those with the mark of the beast are marked for destruction."

"But Holmes, what does 666 mean?"

"Elementary Watson. The mark is the name of the beast, or the number of his name. The name Apollyon means destruction, and the number of his name is the number symbolic of destruction in scripture."

"Brilliant Holmes. The number of the beast Apollyon, whose name means destruction, is 666. This is because Noah was 600 years old when the first destruction came. But Holmes, what of that number I wrote down… The brilliant light in the Hubble Space Photograph being 600,000 times more brilliant than our sun…Could it be a message?"

"Precisely Watson.

Destruction is on the way.

Seek ye the LORD while He may be found.

The Kingdom of Heaven is at Hand."

Advanced Teaching - Symbolism in Revelation chapter 17

Revelation 17:1 *And there came one of the seven angels which had the seven vials, and talked with me, saying unto me, Come hither; I will shew unto thee the judgment of the great whore that sitteth upon many waters:*

"Holmes, What are these waters?"

"All in good time Watson. But first we must proceed."

Revelation 17:3 *So he carried me away in the spirit into the wilderness: and I saw a woman sit upon a scarlet coloured beast, full of names of blasphemy, having seven heads and ten horns.*

"Watson, tell me what the horns on the beast symbolize?"
"I wrote it down Holmes. Horns are spirits."
"Yes Watson, and in this case, demonic spirits… ten fallen angels.
Rulers in the kingdom of darkness in league with the beast Apollyon."

Revelation 17:4 *And the woman was arrayed in purple and scarlet colour, and decked with gold and <u>precious stones</u> and pearls, having a golden cup in her hand full of abominations and filthiness of her fornication:*

A clue from Ezekiel 28..precious stones are on who? The following slides demonstrate Lucifer as the one covered with precious stones.

Ezekiel 28:12 Son of man, take up a lamentation upon the <u>king of Tyrus</u>, and say unto him, Thus saith the Lord GOD; Thou sealest up the sum, full of wisdom, and perfect in beauty.

"Write that down Watson. Note that this culprit Lucifer is AKA king of <u>Tyrus.</u> The ruler over the city which is called the <u>mart of nations</u> which falls to indicate the impending return of Christ.

Ezekiel 28:13 *Thou hast been in Eden the garden of God; <u>every precious stone was thy covering</u>, the sardius, topaz, and the diamond, the beryl, the onyx, and the jasper, the sapphire, the emerald, and the carbuncle, and gold: the workmanship of thy tabrets and of thy pipes was prepared in thee in the day that thou wast created.* ***14*** *Thou art the anointed cherub that covereth; and I have set thee so: thou wast upon the* holy <u>mountain</u> of God; thou hast walked up and down in the midst of the stones of fire.

Note: Another clue…the <u>mountain</u> of God is the <u>Kingdom</u> of God.

"Write that down Watson. Mountain is Kingdom. Whenever we see the word mountain it means kingdom. And remember the clue <u>every precious stone was thy covering</u>."

Ezekiel 28:15 *Thou wast perfect in thy ways from the day that thou wast created, till iniquity was found in thee.* ***16*** *By the multitude of thy merchandise they have filled the midst of thee with violence, and thou hast sinned: therefore I will cast thee as profane out of the* **mountain** *of God: and I will destroy thee, O covering cherub…*

Revelation 17:4 *And the woman was arrayed in purple and scarlet colour, and decked with gold and* <u>precious stones</u> *and pearls, having a golden cup in her hand full of abominations and filthiness of her fornication:*

"Holmes who is this woman of mystery in Revelation chapter 17?"

"Elementary Watson. The woman is covered in precious stones. The woman is Satan. The fallen angel Lucifer. AKA king of Tyrus. AKA king of Babylon or MYSTERY BABYLON."

Revelation 17:5 *And upon her forehead was a name written, MYSTERY, BABYLON THE GREAT, THE MOTHER OF HARLOTS AND ABOMINATIONS OF THE EARTH.*

The identity of the woman is a mystery. Another clue confirming the solution to this mystery is found in the following verses in the book of Revelation speaking of culprit AKA king of Babylon…

Revelation 18:23-24...*for by <u>thy sorceries were all nations deceived</u>. And in her was found the blood of prophets, and of saints, and of all that were slain upon the earth.*

- She is the one responsible for all that were slain on the earth.
- She is the one responsible for **deceiving all nations.**
- The woman is Satan the deceiver of all nations.
- The beast, Apollyon is the DESTROYER.
- The woman Satan aka MYSTERY BABYLON is the DECEIVER.

Another key to the mystery is in ***Revelation 12:9***...*And the great dragon was cast out, that old serpent, called the Devil, and <u>Satan</u>, which <u>deceiveth the whole world</u>: he was cast out into the earth, and his angels were cast out with him.*

Satan is the deceiver of the nations. Satan deceiveth the whole world. And deceived 1/3 of the heavenly angels to rebel against God. The woman is responsible for deceiving all nations. The woman is Satan.

"Watson, Do you think that the other fallen angels who were deceived by Satan want revenge?"

"How should I know Holmes. Is the answer important?"

"We shall see Watson. All in good time".

Revelation 12:6 *And I saw the woman drunken with the blood of the saints, and with the blood of the martyrs of Jesus: and when I saw her, I wondered with great admiration. 7 And the angel said unto me, Wherefore didst thou marvel? I will tell thee the mystery of the woman, and of the beast that carrieth her, which hath the <u>seven heads</u> and ten horns.*

Horns symbolize spirits, what do <u>heads</u> symbolize? We shall see the answer to this important clue later.

Revelation 12:8 *The beast that thou sawest was, and is not; and shall ascend out of the bottomless pit, and go into perdition: and they that dwell on the earth shall wonder, whose names were not written in the book of life from the foundation of the world, when they behold the beast that was, and is not, and yet is.* ***9*** *And here is the mind which hath wisdom. The* <u>*seven heads are seven mountains*</u>*, on which the woman sitteth.*

"Holmes, The seven mountains. They say these are the seven hills of Rome."

"NONSENSE Watson! Mountain is symbolic of Kingdom. The seven mountains are seven kingdoms or in this case seven principalities of a single kingdom."

"What kingdom is that Holmes?"

"Elementary Watson. The Kingdom of Darkness."

Revelation 12:9 *And here is the mind which hath wisdom. The seven heads are seven <u>mountains</u>, on which the woman sitteth...*

To sit on means to preside or reign over. Satan, the woman sits on or presides over seven mountains or principalities in the kingdom of darkness.

Revelation 17:15 *And he saith unto me, The* <u>*waters*</u> *which thou sawest,* <u>*where the whore sitteth*</u>*, are peoples, and multitudes, and nations, and tongues.*

To <u>sit</u> upon or over means to <u>preside or reign</u> over. Satan is called the "god of this world" and reigns over peoples, and multitudes, and nations, and tongues.

2 Corinthians 4:3&4 *But if our gospel be hid, it is hid to them that are lost: In whom <u>the god of this world</u> hath blinded the minds of them which believe not...*

- Satan is the DECEIVER and ruler over the nations of this world system.
- Because Satan is the "god" of this world…
- Satan sits on the waters which symbolize *the peoples, and multitudes, and nations, and tongues* of this world.
- The woman, Satan sits on 7 mountains which are the seven principalities in the kingdom of darkness.
- The word "mountain" signifies kingdom.
- "Mountain" also in this sense carries a meaning of authority or rulership. For example the "mountain of God."
- A mountain is a kingdom or a principality. A principality is a segment of a kingdom over which a prince rules. The kingdom of darkness is divided into seven major principalities. These seven principalities are the mountains on which the woman sits… presides and reigns over.

Note in the following scripture that there are principalities in the kingdom of darkness.

Ephesians 5:12 *For we wrestle not against flesh and blood, but against* **principalities**, *against powers, against the* rulers *of the darkness of this world, against spiritual wickedness in high places.*

- The horns…aka spirit **rulers**
- And heads…aka mountains…aka **principalities**
- The horns or spirit rulers, and the heads or principalities, are a symbolic representation of the entire kingdom of darkness with which we in the kingdom of God wrestle.
- Mountains are kingdoms.
- In this case…the 7 mountains are 7 principalities in the kingdom of darkness over which Satan currently presides or sits.

Revelation 17:9 *And here is the mind which hath wisdom. The seven heads are seven* mountains, *on which the woman sitteth.* **10** *And there are seven kings: five are fallen, and* one is, *and the other* is not *yet come; and when he cometh, he must continue a short space.*

- There are seven kings, one ruler for each principality in the kingdom of darkness.
- "Five are fallen" angels roaming the earth
- "One is…" This means Satan because he still <u>IS</u> by having access to the throne in heaven as the accuser of the brethren…
- The beast is the other who "<u>is not</u>," remember the beast "was, and <u>is not</u>."
- The beast when he comes will continue a short space 42 months. (Rev. 13:5)

Revelation 17:11 *And the beast that was, and is not, even he is the eighth, <u>and is of the seven</u>, and goeth into perdition. **12** And the <u>ten horns</u> which thou sawest are <u>ten kings</u>, which have received no kingdom as yet; but receive power as kings one hour with the beast.*

NOTE: These ten kings are spirit rulers in the kingdom of darkness. They are in league with the beast.

Revelation 17:13 *These have one mind, and shall give their power and strength unto the beast.*

"Holmes. Why do these ten kings, these spirit rulers, give their power and strength to the beast?"

"Elementary Watson. They will help the beast wage <u>two wars</u>. They will win one war and lose the other war. The war they lose will be their last, but is here described first in the next verse."

Revelation 17:14 *These shall make <u>war with the Lamb</u>, and the Lamb shall overcome them: for he is Lord of lords, and King of kings: and they that are with him are called, and chosen, and faithful.*

When they lose this war it will be their last for it is the war described also in Revelation 16:16 (armegeddon) and also described in Revelation 19:19-21 where the beast is ultimately cast into the lake of fire. As a result of this war they loose against the King of kings and Lord of Lords the beast and the false prophet meet their final fate in…

Revelation 19:20 *These both were cast alive into a lake of fire burning with brimstone.*

Revelation 17:15 *And he saith unto me, The waters which thou sawest, where the whore sitteth, are peoples, and multitudes, and nations, and tongues.* ***16*** *And the ten horns which thou sawest upon the beast, these <u>shall hate the whore</u>,*

"Holmes, why do these fallen angels hate the whore Satan?"
"Elementary Watson. Satan deceived them causing them to rebel and be cast out of heaven."

Revelation 17:16 *And the <u>ten horns</u> which thou sawest upon the beast, these <u>shall hate the whore</u>, and shall make her desolate and naked, and shall eat her flesh, and burn her with fire.*

"Watson! A coup de'tat… in the kingdom of darkness!"
This is the other war that the ten horns help the beast wage and they will win this war.

Revelation 17:17 *For God hath put in their hearts to fulfil his will, and to agree, and give their kingdom unto the beast, until the words of God shall be fulfilled.*

Their kingdom, the kingdom of darkness, is taken from Satan and given to the beast Apollyon. He will reign on earth for 42 months as Satan is stripped of all his authority.

- The beast and the ten demonic rulers attack Satan and strip the rule of the kingdom of darkness away from Satan.
- This is part of the judgment of the whore noted in vs. 1 *"Come hither; I will shew unto thee the judgment of the great whore that sitteth upon many waters:"*
- Another part of the judgment of the whore is the destruction of the idol towers of the city of Tyrus or Babylon.

- This is why the announcement that "Babylon is fallen, is fallen" is a pronouncement received with gladness in the kingdom of heaven. It is the declaration that the rule of the king of Tyrus, aka king of Babylon, aka Satan is about to be abolished.
- That is also why the woman Satan, the king of the city, is literally called the city itself in the next verse.

Revelation 17:18 *And the woman which thou sawest is that great city, which reigneth over the kings of the earth.*

Advanced Teaching Symbolism in Revelation Chapter 18

Revelation 18:1 *And after these things I saw another angel come down from heaven, having great power; and the earth was lightened with his glory. 2 And he cried mightily with a strong voice, saying, <u>Babylon the great is fallen, is fallen</u>, and is become the habitation of devils, and the hold of every foul spirit, and a cage of every unclean and hateful bird.*

In the spirit realm the idol towers of Babylon were erected and became the headquarters of many demonic spirits and Satan is the king of this city. Satan is ruler over the merchant city of the world for he is in control of world finance. This is Satan's favorite prinicipality for the love of money is the root of all evil. The pronouncement that the idol towers have fallen is a sign on the earth that the capital of the kingdom of darkness has been demolished.

Revelation 18:3 *For all nations have drunk of the wine of the wrath of her fornication, and the kings of the earth have committed fornication with her, and the merchants of the earth are waxed rich through the abundance of her delicacies. 4 And I heard another voice from heaven, saying, <u>Come out of her, my people</u>, that ye be not partakers of her sins, and that ye receive not of her plagues.*

There were many testimonies after 9-11-01. People reported that God spoke to them and told them to get out and they lived.

Revelation 18:11 *And the merchants of the earth shall weep and mourn over her; for no man buyeth their merchandise any more:*

"Holmes. Why do the merchants weep?"
"Elementary Watson. This city was the center of world trade, a world trade center."

Revelation 18:15 *The merchants of these things, which were made rich by her, shall stand afar off for the fear of her torment, weeping and wailing,* **16** *And saying, Alas, alas, that great city, that was clothed in fine linen, and purple, and scarlet, and decked with gold, and precious stones, and pearls!* **17** *For in one hour so great riches is come to nought. And every shipmaster, and all the company in ships, and sailors, and as many as* **<u>trade</u>** *by sea, stood afar off,* **18** *And cried when they saw the smoke of her burning, saying, What city is like unto this great city!* **19** *And they cast dust on their heads, and cried, weeping and wailing, saying, Alas, alas, that great city, wherein were made rich all that had ships in the sea by reason of her costliness! for in one hour is she made desolate.* **20** *Rejoice over her, thou heaven, and ye holy apostles and prophets; for God hath avenged you on her.* **21** *And a mighty angel took up a stone like a great millstone, and cast it into the sea, saying, Thus with violence shall that great city Babylon be thrown down, and shall be found no more at all…***23****And the light of a candle shall shine no more at all in thee; and the voice of the bridegroom and of the bride shall be heard no more at all in thee: for thy* <u>merchants</u> *were the great men of the earth;*

"Holmes, What type of place would house the greatest merchants on the earth?"
"Elementary Watson. A World Trade Center."

- *for thy merchants were the great men of the earth;*
- *for by thy sorceries were all nations deceived.*

Revelation 18:24 *And in her was found the blood of prophets, and of saints, and of all that were slain upon the earth.*

NOTE: The city houses the great merchants of the earth. The king over the city, Satan, aka king of Tyrus, aka king of Babylon deceived all nations and is responsible for all the slain. In Revelation Chapter 19 after Babylon is fallen what comes next?

Revelation 19:7 *Let us be glad and rejoice, and give honour to him: for the marriage of the Lamb is come, and his wife hath made herself ready. 8 And to her was granted that she should be arrayed in fine linen, clean and white: for the fine linen is the righteousness of saints. 9 And he saith unto me, Write, Blessed are they which are called unto the marriage supper of the Lamb.*

Advanced Teaching Symbolism in Revelation 13

Revelation 13:1 *And I stood upon the sand of the sea, and saw a beast rise up out of the sea, having seven heads and ten horns, and upon his horns ten crowns, and upon his heads the name of blasphemy.*

This is the first of the two fallen angelic beasts to ascend. We know that the two fallen angelic beasts have been locked in the bottomless pit, and when this first beast ascends from the pit he arises out of the sea.

- The heads and horns are symbolic and and this is the same beast with seven heads and ten horns we saw in Revelation ch. 17.
- The identity of the beast is Apollyon.
- The horns represent 10 fallen angelic rulers in league with the beast and the heads represent the 7 principalities in the kingdom of darkness which the beast shall rule when Satan is stripped of his position as we studied.

Note that Satan (the dragon) is described with the same symbolism of having the kingdom of darkness on his head as a crown in...

Revelation 12:3 *And there appeared another wonder in heaven; and behold a great red dragon, having seven heads and ten horns, and seven crowns upon his heads. **4** And his tail drew the third part of the stars of heaven, and did cast them to the earth:*

Also that passage tells of the rebellion of angels...Remember stars=angels.

Revelation 13:2 *And the beast which I saw was like unto a leopard, and his feet were as the feet of a bear, and his mouth as the mouth of a lion:*

Note his actual appearance will be that of a beast or animal creature in the same way the angelic beasts around the throne have the appearance of various animals. This is because he is a fallen angelic beast.

Revelation 13:2*...and the dragon gave him his power, and <u>his seat, and great authority</u>.*
Note: This is not by choice but the result of a coup de'tat in the kingdom of darkness.

Revelation 13:3 *And I saw one of his heads as it were wounded to death;...*

- Note that this is a symbolic death. Remember that heads represent principalities. In other words one of the principalities in the kingdom of darkness suffered a destroying or decimating wound.
- The principality of the world financial system was wounded when the idol towers of Babylon were decimated on 911.
- Two main themes of chapter 13 will be the restoration of this head and the honor of this principality as the beast shall have a

new idol erected to honor him, and shall utterly take command of the world financial system with his mark in that no one shall be able to buy or sell without the mark of the beast…and thus…
- *and his deadly wound was healed:*
- *and all the world wondered after the beast.* **Revelation 13:3**

Revelation 13:4 *And they worshipped the dragon which gave power unto the beast: and they worshipped the beast, saying, Who is like unto the beast? who is able to make war with him?* **5** *And there was given unto him a mouth speaking great things and blasphemies; and power was given unto him to continue forty and two months…* **7** *And it was given unto him to make war with the saints, and to overcome them:*

This appears initially to be a great number. But only that is until we realize that all the saints have escaped to stand before the Son of man at the throne in heaven, with the exception of the two witness which the beast shall ultimately have the power to make war against and kill in Revelation chapter 11.

Revelation 13:7 *…and power was given him over all kindreds, and tongues, and nations.* **8** *And all that dwell upon the earth shall worship him, whose names are not written in the book of life of the Lamb slain from the foundation of the world.*

Those whose names are found in the book of life will not be dwelling on the earth. For if they were still on earth, they also would be deceived by the beast. This deception will not be possible because the angels have evacuated the elect to heaven as seen in Mark 13:22-27.

Revelation 13:11 *And I beheld <u>another beast</u> coming up out of the earth; and he had two horns like a lamb, and he spake as a dragon.* **12** *And he exerciseth all the power of the first beast before him, and causeth the earth and them which dwell therein to worship the first beast,*

Note: The second beast can exercise the same power as the first beast because he also is a fallen angelic beast...An angel of great power and authority.

Revelation 13:13*...And he doeth great wonders, so that he maketh fire come down from heaven on the earth in the sight of men...**14** And deceiveth them that dwell on the earth by the means of those miracles which he had power to do in the sight of the beast; saying to them that dwell on the earth, that they should make an image to the beast,...**15** And he had power to give life unto the image of the beast, that the image of the beast should both speak, and cause that as many as would not worship the image of the beast should be killed.*

- There is no mention of anyone able to resist the two beasts. Remember that they were once angels around the throne with the power to shake the doorposts of the temple of God in heaven.
- Do you think that an unsaved person could stand up to one of them and say... I don't think I will take that mark?
- No, <u>all will take the mark</u> just as it says...

Revelation 13:16 *And he causeth all, both small and great, rich and poor, free and bond, to receive a mark in their right hand, or in their foreheads:*

"Watson the mark is like a brand for branding cattle. If a rancher "<u>causes all</u>" of his cattle to take the mark, do the calves have an option of refusing the mark?"

"No, Holmes they will all take the brand."

"Precisely Watson."

Advanced Teaching Daniel Chapter 9 - Misconceptions of the 70 weeks

"But Holmes, what of the antichrist and the seven year peace treaty with Israel and...and..."

"Nonsense Watson. But here is a clue for you. How long shall the beast, aka the antichrist, aka Apollyon be on the earth?"

"I wrote it down right here Holmes.

42 months. 3 & ½ years after he ascends out of the bottomless pit he will be gone in the lake of fire."

"So Watson, how is it that the beast could make a 7 year peace treaty with Israel, and then after 3 & ½ years break the treaty, take away a fictitious sacrifice, declare himself to be god, and then dominate the earth for another 3 & ½ years?"

"Uh..Uh How so Holmes?"

"Elementary Watson. The whole idea is nonsense. The puzzle of this mystery must be taken apart and put back together properly to get at the truth…"

"But Holmes…"

"Nonsense I say Watson. There will be no seven year peace treaty with Israel. There will be no new temple during tribulation."

"How so Holmes?

"The details are clear Watson as we shall see in Daniel chapter 9. And as for the animal sacrifice that is a mystery for later, The Mystery of The Red Heifer."

Daniel 9:20 *And whiles I was speaking, and praying, and confessing my sin and the sin of my people Israel, and presenting my supplication before the LORD my God for the holy mountain of my God;*

Note: The mountain of God is the kingdom of God.

Daniel 9:21 *Yea, whiles I was speaking in prayer, even the man Gabriel, whom I had seen in the vision at the beginning, being caused to fly swiftly, touched me about the time of the evening oblation.* **22** *And he informed me, and talked with me, and said, O Daniel, I am now come forth to give thee skill and understanding…* **24** *Seventy weeks are determined upon thy people and upon thy holy city,*

- The people of Daniel are the children of Israel.
- The holy city is the city of Jerusalem.
- The seventy weeks are determined on Israel and Jerusalem.
- Events in the gentile world will not be considered when counting the 70 weeks.
- Jesus 3 & ½ year ministry on earth was exclusively to the Jews.
- But from the time of the cross, where Jesus once and for all was sacrificed for the sins of the whole world, until now… that time is not counted in the 70 weeks which refer exclusively to the nation of Israel.

Daniel 9:24 *Seventy weeks are determined upon thy people and upon thy holy city, to finish the transgression, and to make an end of sins, and to make reconciliation for iniquity, and to bring in everlasting righteousness, and to seal up the vision and prophecy, and to anoint the most Holy.*

…to finish the transgression, and to make an end of sins, and to make reconciliation for iniquity, and to bring in everlasting righteousness,… These have been accomplished by Jesus at the cross.

The anointing of the most Holy was accomplished with the Spirit of the Lord coming down upon Jesus as a dove to anoint Jesus at his baptism. This began the 3 &1/2 year ministry of the Messiah Prince Jesus Christ to the Jews.

Daniel 9:25 *Know therefore and understand, that from the going forth of the commandment to restore and to build Jerusalem unto the Messiah the Prince shall be seven weeks, and threescore and two weeks:*

A total of 69 weeks of years. 69 weeks from the command to restore and build Jerusalem unto the Messiah the Prince. 69 X 7 = 483 years.

This was the time to the point when Jesus was anointed as Messiah Prince at his baptism when the Holy Spirit descended upon him and he began his ministry. Why is the time divided into 7 weeks and then 62 weeks? Let's look again.

Daniel 9:25 *Know therefore and understand, that from the going forth of the commandment to restore and to build Jerusalem unto the Messiah the Prince shall be <u>seven weeks</u>, and <u>threescore and two weeks</u>:*

- In the first seven weeks or 49 years the temple was rebuilt. <u>After the first seven weeks</u>, came <u>the next 62</u> weeks or 434 years.
- There were 434 years from the point the temple was rebuilt until the arrival on earth of <u>the ministry of Messiah the Prince</u>.

Daniel 9:26 *And <u>after</u> threescore and two weeks shall Messiah be cut off, but not for himself:*

Note: Note at a point in time after the 62 weeks which comes after the 7 weeks then Messiah shall be cut off or killed not for himself but for the sins of the world.

Daniel 9:26 *And after threescore and two weeks shall Messiah be cut off, but not for himself: and the people of the **prince** <u>that shall come</u> shall destroy the city and the sanctuary;*

"Which prince Holmes?"
"Elementary Watson. The Messiah Prince sent a people to destroy the city and sanctuary. This is just as Jesus prophesied in Matthew 24:2

Matthew 24:2*…verily I say unto you, There shall not be left here one stone upon another, that shall not be thrown down.*

"Why was the temple destroyed Holmes?"
"Elementary Watson. Destruction of the temple and a near two millennium exile of the Jews came because of their <u>rejection of the Messiah Prince Jesus Christ</u>."

- Due to their rejection of Jesus the Messiah Prince…
- The demonic forces of the Roman army were unleashed in judgement.

- The Roman army was God's instrument of judgement.
- To bring total destruction of the Temple.

Daniel 9:26 *...and the people of the prince that shall come shall destroy the city and the sanctuary; and the end thereof shall be with a flood, and <u>unto the end of the war</u> desolations are determined.*

"Until the end of which war Holmes?"

"That's the correct question Watson. It is the war with the kingdom of darkness. Desolation of the temple is determined until the end of the war with the kingdom of darkness. The temple can never be rebuilt until the end of the war with the kingdom of darkness which will not be completed until after the tribulation period is completely over and gone."

Daniel 9:27 *And he shall <u>confirm the covenant</u> with many for one week:*

"Holmes, is this not the peace treaty with the antichrist?"
"Nonsense Watson. Look at the grammar."

Daniel 9:27 *And **he** shall confirm the covenant with many for one week:*

- A pronoun must refer to a prior noun in the text.
- Who is the <u>he</u>?
- The he can only refer back once again to the <u>Messiah Prince</u> and the <u>Covenant</u> he confirms with the nation of Israel. This is a HOLY Covenant. It is not a covenant of the antichrist.
- The <u>Holy</u> Covenant is also specifically seen also three times in Daniel chapter 11 in verses 28-30. The Holy Covenant is a covenant of the Lord and is a covenant of the blood of Jesus Christ. It is not a peace treaty the antichrist makes with Israel.
- But in the midst of the week <u>he,</u> the Messiah Prince permanently puts an end to animal sacrifice with his own death on the cross. Jesus Christ caused the animal sacrificial system according to the law to cease.

Daniel 9:27 *And <u>he</u> shall confirm the covenant with many for one week: and in the midst of the week he shall cause the sacrifice and the oblation to cease,*

- The pronoun "<u>he</u>" refers back to <u>Messiah the Prince</u>
- The Messiah Prince takes away the first sacrificial system of sacrificing the blood of an animal causing it to cease by the offering of his own body, the body of Jesus Christ once for all.

Hebrews 10:9-10*...He taketh away the first, that he may establish the second. By the which will we are sanctified through the offering of the body of Jesus Christ once for all.*

Jesus the Messiah Prince is the one who at the cross has permanently taken away the sacrifice to be offered by the law.

"But, But HOLMES, how can the Holy covenant be confirmed by Jesus to Israel for one week of <u>seven years</u> when Jesus was crucified in the middle of the week after only <u>3 & ½ years</u> of his ministry to the Jews? Where is the missing ½ week or 3 & ½ years?"

"Elementary Watson. The remnant of Israel 144,000 will be taken on the day of the Lord to a place in the wilderness and nourished there for 3 & ½ years as seen in Revelation 12:14. But this is the mystery. What will they be fed Watson?"

"Will it be Manna Holmes?"

"Elementary Watson. They shall be fed the Word of God and Zechariah 12:10 shall be fulfilled."

Zechariah 12:10 *...and they shall look upon me whom they have pierced, and they shall mourn for him, as one mourneth for his only son, and shall be in bitterness for him, as one that is in bitterness for his firstborn.*

- And the Messiah Prince will finish confirming the Holy Covenant exclusively with the remnant of the nation of Israel for

the second half of the seventieth week of Daniel during the 3 & ½ year tribulation period on earth.
- This will occur at a mystery location which has been prepared for them in the wilderness.

Daniel 9:27 *And he shall confirm the covenant with many for one week: and in the midst of the week he shall cause the sacrifice and the oblation to cease, and for the overspreading of abominations he shall make it desolate, even until the consummation, and that determined shall be poured upon the desolate.*

- To review above…*and for the overspreading of abominations he shall make it desolate, even until the consummation, and that determined shall be poured upon the desolate.*
- He once again refers to Messiah…
- and due to the overspreading rejection of Messiah he shall make the temple desolate to the consumation i.e. to the end…

Daniel 9:27 *…and for the overspreading of abominations he shall make it desolate, even until the consummation, and that determined shall be poured upon the desolate.*

- This overspreading abomination is the widespread rejection by the Jews of Messiah. Not his crucifixion, but rather the overspreading unbelief in the sin cleansing power of His sacrificial blood.
- Daniel confirms that he shall make it, the temple desolate to the consumation…the very end.
- And it is determined also that Israel shall enter their longest and most harsh exile after their rejection of the Messiah Prince Jesus Christ.

"A question Watson. Do you think Jesus would want the Jews to continue to make animal sacrifices at the temple for the cleansing of their sins after He shed his own blood once and for all?"

"Of course not Holmes."

"Precisely Watson. Is it any mystery that the temple was destroyed? Write this down Watson.It is a clue to our next mystery. Desolation came to the temple and to the Jews because of their rejection of the blood of Jesus Christ. Rejection of the blood of Christ and trusting elsewhere for the forgiveness of sins is IDOLATRY."

Advanced Teaching The Abomination of Desolation

Matthew 24:14 And of this gospel of the Kingdom shall be preached in all the world for a witness unto all nations; and then shall the end come. 15 When ye <u>therefore</u> shall see the ABOMINATION OF DESOLATION, spoken of by Daniel the prophet, stand in the holy place, (whoso readeth, let him understand:)... 16 Then let them which be in Judaea flee into the mountains... 17 Let him which is on the housetop not come down to take any thing out of his house...18 Neither let him which is in the field return back to take his clothes...21 For <u>then shall be great tribulation</u>, such as was not since the beginning of the world to this time, no, nor ever shall be.

- The abomination of desolation shall occur on the day of the Lord.
- On the same day that the angel preaches the everlasting gospel to every ear on earth…
- *"…in all the world for a witness unto all nations…"*
- Then those in Judea of Israel are instructed to <u>flee to the mountains</u>...
- Note a clue. The first mountain nearest and east of Jerusalem is the <u>Mount of Olives</u>.
- Then is the beginning of tribulation.

Mystery of the abomination of desolation

Matthew 24:15 When ye therefore shall see the abomination of desolation, spoken of by Daniel the prophet, stand in the holy place, **<u>(whoso readeth, let him understand)</u>**...

Review of some events on the day of the Lord.
- Angel preaches to all nations.
- Abomination of Desolation seen in the Holy Place.

- Jews are to flee to the mountains.
- Then is the start of tribulation.

Matthew 24:14 *And of this gospel of the Kingdom shall be preached in all the world for a witness unto all nations; and then shall the end come.* **15** *When ye therefore shall see the ABOMINATION OF DESOLATION, spoken of by Daniel the prophet, stand <u>in the holy place</u>, (whoso readeth, let him understand:)* **16** *Then let them which be in Judae-a flee into the mountains:* **17** *Let him which is upon the housetop not come down to take anything out of his house:* **18** *Neither let him which is in the field return back to take his clothes.* **19** *And woe unto them that are with child, and to them that give suck in those days!* **20** *But pray ye that your <u>flight</u> be not in the winter, neither on the sabbath day:*

(Note: This shall be the flight into the wilderness of the 144,000 Jews.)

21 *For then shall be great tribulation, such as was not since the beginning of the world to this time, no, nor ever shall be.*

- The Holy Place is a location of the temple mount where the Jews would like to rebuild the temple.
- The prototype of the abomination of desolation is described in Daniel chapter 11.
- The events which transpired as Daniel prophesied are known to be fact in historical accounts.
- The prototype of the abomination of desolation occured when the ancient king Antiochus Epiphanes conquered Jerusalem.
- This king, went to the holy place, entered the temple and ransacked it.

- He set up an Idol to Zeus
- Then he sacrificed the blood of the biggest fattest pig he could find.
- The pig was by the law of God an unclean animal totally unacceptable as a blood sacrifice.
- This was an open blasphemous affront to the proper sacrifice God had ordained for the Jews.
- Who were to offer acceptable blood sacrifices according to the law of God for the cleansing of sin.

- These events, the idolatry and blasphemous blood sacrifice were the occasion of the abomination of desolation and were the fulfillment of the abomination of desolation Daniel prophesied in Daniel chapter 11.
- What will be the abomination of desolation?
- We must look for the clue in the book of Hebrews.

Hebrews 10:4 *For it is not possible that the blood of bulls and of goats should take away sins.*

Hebrews 10:8 *Above when he said, Sacrifice and offering and burnt offerings and offering for sin thou wouldest not, neither hadst pleasure therein; which are offered by the law;*

Hebrews 10:9-10 *Then said he, Lo, I come to do thy will, O God.*
He taketh away the first, that he may establish the second.
By the which will we are sanctified...
...through the offering of the body of Jesus Christ...
...once for all.

"But Holmes. How could the abomination of desolation occur since that the sacrifice of animals for the forgiveness of sin has been done away with? What would constitute idolatry and a blasphemous blood sacrifice at the site of the Holy Place?"

"Elementary Watson. Idolatry will be the setting up of an altar at the site of the Holy Place to sacrifice the now unacceptable blood of an animal as a blasphemous affront to the blood of Jesus."

The solution is in the mystery of the red heifer.

On video screen is Cover of the book

<u>Mystery of the Red Heifer Devine Promise of Purity</u>

by Rabbi Chaim Richman

"Watson tell me, is the red heifer our devine promise of purity?"

"Of course not Holmes, the blood of Jesus Christ is our only source of purity and forgiveness of sins. Like you say Holmes. It is elementary."

"Precisely Watson. But there is a red heifer that will be sacrificed. And the mystery of the red heifer sacrifice indicates that the time of the end is near."

The following quote was obtained from the website http://members.ozemail.com.au/~adamgosp/heifer.htm

"NEWS FLASH: Red Heifer Born in Israel! In these days of difficulty for the Land of Israel, there is encouraging news as well... It can now be revealed that less than one month ago, a red heifer was born in Israel. After the heifer's owner contacted the Temple Institute, on Friday, <u>April 5th, 2002</u>, Rabbi Menachem Makover and Rabbi Chaim Richman traveled to the farm where the heifer is located, to inspect and validate her status. The rabbis found her to be kosher and were satisfied that this heifer could indeed be a candidate to be used in the process of purification described in the book of Numbers, chapter 19. This is a prerequisite for the rebuilding of the Holy Temple. Tradition records that a red heifer in our generation is a herald of the Messianic era."

The following information is from an article by Rod Dreher in the National Review on April 11, 2002

http://www.nationalreview.com/dreher/dreher041102.asp

April 11, **2002** 8:30 a.m.

Red-Heifer Days an article by Rod Dreher

National Review

An article by Rod Dreher in the National Review reveals detail regarding the historical and geopolitical importance of the red heifer and the turmoil that would surround the ritual sacrifice of the red heifer. Many details of the red heifer are contained in this article which can be seen at the website...

http://www.nationalreview.com/dreher/dreher041102.asp

According to Dreher a calf was born in 2002 that rabbis examined and declared to be ritually acceptable for the red heifer sacrifice. The calf would be required to reach the mandated age of three years and remain spotless and of perfect color.

Dreher writes... *"So how does the calf recently born in Israel figure into things? As Gorenberg explains, the ashes of a flawless red heifer —*

an extremely rare creature — were required by the ancient Hebrews to purify worshipers who went into the Temple to pray. In modern times, rabbinical law forbids Jews from setting foot on the Temple Mount, thus violating the site where the Holy of Holies dwelled, until and unless they are ritually purified. Without a perfect red heifer to sacrifice, the Third Temple cannot be built, and Moshiach — the Messiah — will not come. Writes Gorenberg, "[Israeli] government officials and military leaders could only regard the requirement for the missing heifer as a stroke of sheer good fortune preventing conflict over the Mount."

Dreher goes on to explain the geopolitical significance... "David Landau, columnist for the Israeli daily Haaretz. He called the red heifer "a four-legged bomb" that could "set the entire region on fire." Muslim leaders worried about the red heifer too, as they would see an attempt by Jews to take over the Temple Mount as a sign of the Islamic apocalypse."

- The red heifer in the story reached the age of sacrifice 3 years in March 2005.
- According to an unconfirmed source at the Temple Institute in Israel...
- there are a number of candidates for the red heifer
- but they stated that they could give no further information regarding the red heifer.
- The red heifer must be sacrificed outside the camp and the ashes taken to the Holy Place for purification of sins in order for the priests to set up the altar for animal sacrifice at the site of the Holy Place.
- The temple does not have to rebuilt, merely the cornerstone laid, and the altar set up for animal sacrifice to begin at the Holy Place.
- With help of the Israeli military these events could suddenly all transpire within hours on the temple mount.
- The setting up of an altar for animal sacrifice will constituting <u>idolatry</u>, and the <u>blasphemous shedding of the blood</u> of an animal for the forgiveness of sins are the events that will be seen on the temple mount constituting the <u>abomination of desolation</u>.

"But Holmes how does the sacrifice of the red heifer and the setting up of an altar for animal sacrifice fit with the events of the day of the Lord?"

"Elementary Watson. When the blood of Jesus was shed on the cross the outpouring of the <u>grace of God was poured out upon the earth</u>. Three events transpired with the shedding of the blood of Jesus."

- The sun went dark Luke 23:45
- There was a great earthquake and the rocks were rent. Matt. 27:51
- The resurrection of many of the dead also occurred. Matt. 27:52
- When the altar is set up and the unacceptable blood of an animal is shed by the Jews
- the outpouring of <u>the wrath of God shall pour out upon the earth</u>.
- The same three events shall be seen and are events of the day of the Lord.
- The sun will go dark
- A great earthquake will shake every mountain and island
- And the resurrection of the dead in Christ
- Followed by the rapture of the church.

Advanced Teaching - Preservation of the remnant of Israel - Zechariah 12 & 14

"Holmes, when the Jews take the temple mount and set up an altar, won't that start world war?"

"Precisely Watson. Jerusalem will come under immediate attack. Jesus instructed the Jews when they see the abomination of desolation to flee to the mountains. The first mountain outside of Jerusalem they come to will be the mount of Olives. Jesus will appear to them there and shall provide for their escape into the wilderness as the mount of Olives splits forming a valley for their escape. And they shall look upon Him who they have pierced and weep..."

Painting entitled They Shall Mourn for Him by Larissa Lando

Zechariah 12:10 *And I will pour upon the house of David, and upon the inhabitants of Jerusalem, the spirit of grace and of supplications: and they shall look upon me whom they have pierced, and they shall mourn for him, as one mourneth for his only son, and shall be in bitterness for him, as one that is in bitterness for his firstborn.*

Zechariah 14:1 *Behold,* **the day of the LORD** *cometh, and thy spoil shall be divided in the midst of thee.* ***2*** *For I will gather all nations against Jerusalem to battle; and the city shall be taken,...*

Zechariah 14:3 *Then shall the LORD go forth, and fight against those nations, as when he fought in the day of battle.*

Zechariah 14:4 **And his feet shall stand in that day upon the mount of Olives**, *and the mount of Olives shall cleave in the midst thereof toward the east and toward the west, and there shall be a very great valley; and half of the mountain shall remove toward the north, and half of it toward the south.*

Zechariah 14:5 *And* <u>ye shall flee to the valley</u> *of the mountains...*

Events of <u>the day of the Lord.</u>
- Jerusalem is under attack.
- Jesus stands on the Mount of Olives.
- The mount of Olives splits forming a valley.
- The children of Israel flee though the valley of the mountain into the wilderness for protection.

THESE EVENTS OCCUR AT THE ONSET OF TRIBULATION NOT THE END OF TRIBULATION.

The children of Israel flee Jerusalem to a place in the wilderness to be nourished there for 3 & ½ years. They flee at the onset of tribulation not at the end of tribulation.

Painting depicting the escape of the children of Israel fleeing through the valley of the mountain. Zechariah 14:5 by Larissa Lando

"Holmes, what is the destination of the 144,000 fleeing through this valley?"

"Elementary Watson. To a place prepared in the wilderness where they shall be nourished and protected by God for the 3&1/2 year tribulation."

"But Holmes, what is this mysterious place prepared for the children of Israel?"

"Elementary Watson. You see the Mount of Olives is on the east of Jerusalem. The Mount of Olives will split under the feet of Jesus on the day of the Lord forming a long valley going east and west. West would lead back to Jerusalem which will be under attack. Thus they shall flee <u>to the east</u> through the valley."

"But Holmes what about the ancient fortified city of Petra? Are they going to Petra?"

"Nonsense Watson. Petra is south they will be heading <u>east</u>. If we were to travel east from Jerusalem we would eventually come to the area of two rivers, the Tigris and the Euphrates. In Genesis Chapter 2 we note that the location of the Garden of Eden was near four rivers, two of which are the Euphrates and the Hiddekel now known as the Tigris.

When Adam and Eve were forced to leave the garden, two angels and a flaming sword were placed to stand guard. And this is the clue Watson. There is no need to guard something that has no future use. If there is no future use, it could have been destroyed. The Garden of Eden lies east of Jerusalem and has been under angelic guard."

"HOLMES BRILLIANT! The Garden of Eden! But Holmes, could it really be the Garden of Eden?"

"All in good time Watson. We shall see. All in good time."

**DON'T MISS
THE ONLINE STREAMING VIDEO
TEACHING SERIES
MYSTERIES OF REVELATION UNVEILED**
by Dr. Terry Gage
at www.biblemystery.com

www.ingramcontent.com/pod-product-compliance
Lightning Source LLC
Chambersburg PA
CBHW070558100426
42744CB00006B/324